D1153183

C/YPC/04

An Anglican Companion

O Lord God,
from whom we come,
in whom we are enfolded,
to whom we shall return:
Bless us in our pilgrimage through life;
with the power of the Father protecting,
with the love of Jesus indwelling,
and the light of the Spirit guiding,
until we come to our ending,
in life and love eternal.

The Bishop's Pilgrimage Prayer for
the Norwich diocese, 1995
The Rt Revd Peter Nott

An Anglican Companion

WORDS FROM THE HEART OF FAITH

COMPILED BY
Alan Wilkinson
and
Christopher Cocksworth

CHURCH HOUSE PUBLISHING

This edition first published 2001 in Great Britain
by SPCK and Church House Publishing

The Society for Promoting Christian Knowledge
Holy Trinity Church
Marylebone Road
London
NW1 4DU

Church House Publishing
Church House
Great Smith Street
London
SW1P 3NZ

Second impression 2002

British Library Cataloguing in Publication Data

A catalogue record for this book is available from
the British Library.

ISBN 0-281-05359-6 (SPCK)
      0-7151-3785-9 (CHP)

Typeset by Pioneer Associates, Perthshire
Printed in Great Britain by
Mackays of Chatham

Contents

Preface

As they embark on the Christian journey, people who are beginning to pray need a basic diet to shape and feed their prayer. There is need for a Companion to nourish and help them in their prayers, small enough to go into a pocket and rich enough in resources to last a lifetime.

This volume offers that richness, drawing its prayers from many sources – English and worldwide. It provides the basic diet to sustain personal prayer in the Church, providing those texts which we should all know by heart, and introducing its users to the concept of a disciplined pattern of prayer; there is a fourteen-day cycle of daily prayer under the heading 'Prayer for today'.

New Anglicans – and many who have been members of the Church of England for some time – will be grateful to Canon Alan Wilkinson and Dr Christopher Cocksworth and the representative group supporting them.

While primarily designed for new members of the Church, there is much of value here for all Christians, and we hope that it will rapidly gain a central place in the praying life of the Church. Running through the rich diversity of the Church of England is a central core of disciplined prayer, built around prayers we have in common, which form the backbone of our worship.

Wide use of this Companion will help to reinforce the common prayer which binds us together at all stages of our journey to God. We welcome this new edition, which has been revised to bring it into line with the changes brought to the liturgy by *Common Worship*, and we commend it for widespread use.

George Carey, Archbishop of Canterbury
David Hope, Archbishop of York

A short guide to the duties of Church membership for members of the Church of England

As baptised and confirmed members of our Church, we are called upon to play a full part in its life and witness. That means we should:

> Follow the example of Christ in home and daily life, and seek to grow in faith.
>
> Read and study the Bible prayerfully.
>
> Celebrate together in Sunday and weekday worship God's love for the world.
>
> Receive the Holy Communion faithfully and regularly.
>
> Pray daily for the coming of God's kingdom of justice, mercy and peace, seeking to promote the common good by prayer and example.
>
> Express our Christian faith in work and leisure; in the life of our neighbourhood and nation; in our concern for the peoples of the world and the future of the earth.
>
> Dedicate our personal gifts and talents to Christ in the service of the Church and the community.
>
> Give generously for the work of the Church at home and overseas, and for other charitable causes.
>
> Support Christian values, especially relating to marriage, children, family, neighbours and community.

George Carey, Archbishop of Canterbury
David Hope, Archbishop of York

Notes on compilers

Alan Wilkinson, a Visiting Lecturer at Portsmouth University, was formerly Diocesan Theologian at Portsmouth Cathedral. He is the author of two books about the churches and the wars; he also wrote the history of the Community of the Resurrection. His latest book is *Christian Socialism, Scott Holland to Tony Blair*. He contributes to a number of periodicals including the *Church Times*.

Christopher Cocksworth, Principal of Ridley Hall Theological College, Cambridge, is a member of the Church of England Liturgical Commission and the Group for the Renewal of Worship (GROW). He is the author of *Evangelical Eucharistic Thought in the Church of England, Holy, Holy, Holy: Worshipping the Trinitarian God* and various other publications on Christian worship.

Introduction

At one time each Christian tradition held a store of religious writings which its followers could draw upon both for regular use and in emergencies. For Anglicans this store included some well-known hymns and passages from the Bible, some psalms and collects from the Book of Common Prayer, and parts of spiritual classics such as *Pilgrim's Progress*. Many learned this material by heart at home, in Sunday school and day school, so it was readily available. Edwin Muir, the twentieth-century Scottish poet, wandered away from his early Christian faith. But in 1939, when middle aged, he began to return to faith through rediscovering the Lord's Prayer which he had learned as a child in the Orkneys:

> Last night, going to bed alone, I suddenly found myself... reciting the Lord's Prayer in a loud emphatic voice – a thing I had not done for many years – with deep urgency and profound disturbed emotion. While I went on I grew more composed; as if it had been empty and craving and were being replenished, my soul grew still; every word had a strange fullness of meaning which astonished and delighted me.
>
> *Edwin Muir, An Autobiography*

Terry Waite, during his years as a hostage, was able to recall large parts of the Prayer Book from his time as a choirboy 40 years previously. So most mornings he said the words of the Communion Service silently from memory; at night he would say Evensong in the same way. Afterwards he sometimes felt better; mostly he felt little difference: 'The prayers, however, helped me to find a structure in my solitary day and helped me to look outside myself towards God. I was learning how unwise it is to depend too much on feelings' (*Footfalls in Memory*).

Since Terry Waite's boyhood there have been many changes in society, education and the Church. As a result, many Anglicans no longer have a common store upon which to draw. *An Anglican Companion* attempts to fill that gap. It is like a knapsack, small enough to be carried on the back, but large enough to contain all the basic necessities for a journey.

We have not attempted to argue the case for Christianity, or for life as a pilgrimage to the heavenly city – there are plenty of other books which do that. Rather we have created the *Companion* for all interested in finding out more about 'The Way' (as Christianity is called in Acts), for those venturing out (perhaps nervously), as well as for those already confidently striding along the road; for those preparing for baptism and confirmation (at whatever age) and beginning the Christian life; for parents being challenged by the prospect of their child's baptism or confirmation; for couples getting married; for groups of Christians exploring the faith; for those at one of the many turning points of life; for the sick and housebound; for those going into hospital; for groups or individuals wanting to learn to pray; for those who are growing older or preparing to die.

The *Companion* is designed to be read slowly and reflectively so that it is absorbed into the heart as well as the mind. It is not intended to be read through at a sitting, but savoured, a small portion at a time. You might use it for your daily prayers, or turn to it at some crisis or crossroads, or use it regularly for meditation as you travel to work.

The *Companion* is divided into four sections, each with its own introduction:

1 'Walking the way of Christ' – four Key Texts which every Christian should know.

2 'Prayer for today' – a form of daily prayer and Bible readings.

3 'Changing scenes of life' – passages for the various stages of life, arranged in sequence.

4 'Sharing in the company' – the life of the Church: its teaching; its fellowship; the Eucharist; ways of prayer. This section could be used as an outline preparation for baptism and confirmation or as an outline refresher course on belief and practice.

We have drawn upon The Book of Common Prayer (1662), *Common Worship* (2000) and a wide range of other material, ancient and modern. And we have used, unless we have said otherwise, The New Revised Standard Version for biblical passages.

In preparation of the first edition we were deeply grateful for the support of the Archbishops of Canterbury and York, the Bishop of St Edmundsbury and Ipswich, the Bishop of Salisbury and the House of Bishops; representatives of the Board of Mission and Unity, the Board of Education and the Liturgical Commission; Rachel Boulding then of SPCK, Alan Mitchell of Church House Publishing and also many individuals who made helpful suggestions. In this second edition, as well as bringing the liturgical material into conformity with *Common Worship*, we have made a few alterations and additions. Once again we are grateful to the staff of SPCK and CHP for their support and assistance.

Alan Wilkinson
Christopher Cocksworth

List of abbreviations

AV   Authorized Version

BCP   The Book of Common Prayer (1662)

CCP   *Celebrating Common Prayer, A Version of the Daily Office SSF*, Mowbray, 1992

CW   *Common Worship: Services and Prayers for the Church of England*, CHP, 2000

HAM   *Hymns Ancient and Modern Revised New Standard*, The Canterbury Press, 1983

NEH   *The New English Hymnal*, The Canterbury Press, 1986

NIV   New International Version

NRSV   New Revised Standard Version

REB   Revised English Bible

RSV   Revised Standard Version

An explanation of the terms used in the *Companion* can be found in *The Church of England A-Z: A Glossary of Terms* (Church House Publishing, 1994).

PART ONE

Walking the way of Christ

Part One: Walking the way of Christ

'Keep these words that I am commanding you today in your heart' (Deuteronomy 6.6) – so God's people of old were told as they journeyed to the promised land. Part One of the *Companion* consists of four important texts which the Church invites us to 'keep in our hearts' so that we can draw on them as we walk the way of Christ.

Key texts

These four texts have played a key part in forming the identity and character of Christians throughout the life of the Church. They are some of the basic rations for our journey of faith. They can help us most when we become very familiar with them. It is good to know them by heart so that they are always available to us. Each one focuses on a different aspect of our baptism into the way of Christ. 'Repent, and be baptised every one of you in the name of Jesus Christ so that your sins may be forgiven; and you will receive the gift of the Holy Spirit.' (Acts 2. 38)

In baptism we are called to **worship** God in lives of love:

> **Our Lord Jesus Christ said:**
> **The first commandment is this:**
> **'Hear, O Israel, the Lord our God is the only Lord.**
> **You shall love the Lord your God with all your heart,**
> **with all your soul, with all your mind,**
> **and with all your strength.'**
>
> **The second is this: 'Love your neighbour as yourself.'**
> **There is no other commandment greater than these.**
> **On these two commandments hang all the law and the**
> **prophets.**

The Summary of the Law: Mark 12. 29–31

In baptism we are called to **pray** as Jesus taught us:

Our Father in heaven,	Our Father, who art in heaven,
hallowed be your name,	hallowed by thy name;
your kingdom come,	thy kingdom come;
your will be done,	thy will be done;
on earth as in heaven.	on earth as it is in heaven.
Give us today our daily	Give us this day our daily
bread.	bread.
Forgive us our sins	And forgive us our trespasses,
as we forgive those	as we forgive those
who sin against us.	who trespass against us.
Lead us not into	And lead us not into
temptation	temptation;
but deliver us from evil.	but deliver us from evil.
For the kingdom, the power,	For thine is the kingdom,
and the glory are yours	the power and the glory,
now and for ever.	for ever and ever.
Amen.	Amen.
The Lord's Prayer, contemporary	*The Lord's Prayer, traditional*

In baptism we are called to **hear** the teaching of Scripture and to **share** the faith of the Church:

I believe in God, the Father almighty,
creator of heaven and earth.

I believe in Jesus Christ, his only Son, our Lord,
who was conceived by the Holy Spirit,
born of the Virgin Mary,
suffered under Pontius Pilate,
was crucified, died, and was buried;
he descended to the dead.
On the third day he rose again;
he ascended into heaven,
he is seated at the right hand of the Father,
and he will come to judge the living and the dead.

I believe in the Holy Spirit,
the holy catholic Church,
the communion of saints,
the forgiveness of sins,
the resurrection of the body,
and the life everlasting.
Amen.

The Apostles' Creed

In baptism we are called to **live** the lifestyle of Christ:

**Blessed are the poor in spirit,
for theirs is the kingdom of heaven.**

**Blessed are those who mourn,
for they shall be comforted.**

**Blessed are the meek,
for they shall inherit the earth.**

**Blessed are those who hunger and thirst after
    righteousness,
for they shall be satisfied.**

**Blessed are the merciful,
for they shall obtain mercy.**

**Blessed are the pure in heart,
for they shall see God.**

**Blessed are the peacemakers,
for they shall be called children of God.**

**Blessed are those who suffer persecution for
    righteousness' sake,
for theirs is the kingdom of heaven.**

The Beatitudes: Matthew 5. 3–10

PART TWO

Prayer for today

Part Two: Prayer for today

God's people have known that if they are to walk in his way, they need the daily nourishment which comes from spending time with God in prayer and in listening to the Scriptures. Part Two of the *Companion* provides a simple framework and some tried and tested material to help sustain and deepen our fellowship with God, through Jesus his Son and by the power of the Spirit.

Christians have spent their daily time with God in many different ways over the centuries. But often the various forms of prayer have had a simple structure, like the one which follows, and have used common texts, many of which you will find here. This way of praying is known as the Daily Office. After using this form for some time you may like to move on to one of the fuller versions of the Office found in *BCP*, *CCP* or *CW*.

Before beginning to use this part of the *Companion* you will find it helpful to read the next two pages which explain how to make the best use of this form of prayer.

A fortnight's daily prayer

On the left hand side of the page you will find the day of the week indicated, alongside the theme of the day. Then you will see three sections – PREPARING, HEARING and RESPONDING.

In the PREPARING section a short text is given. This may be some verses from a psalm or a hymn, a prayer or a piece of the liturgy. It is there to help you enter into the presence of God. It is only a starter – you may want to add other prayers to it or spend some time in silence. In addition, you may want to light a candle, make the sign of the cross or lift up your hands so as to acknowledge God's presence and to express your willingness to receive from him.

In the HEARING section you will find a short reading from the Bible. Even though it may be a familiar passage to you, try not to rush your way through. Rather, take time over it and allow God to speak to you. After using this reading for a number of times you may want to try one of the alternative ones (on pp. 42–3) or choose one from elsewhere in the *Companion* for a change of diet.

In the RESPONDING section you have the chance to respond to God by reflecting on the reading, by praising and by praying. Here you can draw on your own words, from material **on the right hand side of the page**, from other parts of the *Companion* or from other sources which you find helpful. Some guidance is given about areas to pray for on particular days. Further guidance is available on pp. 112–14 about different ways of praying and praising. It would be worth turning to this, especially in those times when you find prayer difficult. A collect is given as a way of gathering our prayers around the theme of the day and the Lord's Prayer is suggested as the way of bringing the prayers to a close. This family prayer of the Church reminds us that all our praying, even if it is taking place in our most private moments, is always a sharing in the prayer of the whole Church. As well as joining us with Christians throughout the world, it links us with Jesus' first disciples and his followers of every age.

You may like to conclude this daily time with God by saying:

The grace of our Lord Jesus Christ,
and the love of God,
and the fellowship of the Holy Spirit,
be with us all evermore. Amen.

On the right hand side of the page there is some 'more material for prayer and praise'. Each day you will find two or three texts drawn from across the centuries – psalms from our Jewish forebears in the faith; canticles (or scriptural songs) of the universal Church; prayers from great Christian individuals and from the public liturgy of the Church of England; hymns of praise from the early to recent days of the Church.

This material is for you to use as you choose. Generally you will find it suitable for the RESPONDING section but you may want to use at least one in the PREPARING section. Do not feel that you have to use this material every time. It is simply there to supplement the diet. Sometimes you may like to use both texts, sometimes just one and at other times none. It is important to feel relaxed and to be flexible about the amount of material you use.

As a way of concluding a psalm or canticle you may like to say:

Glory to the Father and to the Son
and to the Holy Spirit;
as it was in the beginning is now
and shall be for ever. Amen.

Remember that the Key Texts (on pp. 4–7) are always there for you to draw upon in your prayer and praise.

In total 14 forms of prayer are provided, one for each day of the week over a two-week period:

Sunday	Meeting the risen Christ	Worshipping God in the risen Christ
Monday	Celebrating God's work in creation	Receiving God's life through the Spirit
Tuesday	Waiting for the coming of Christ	Welcoming the light of Christ
Wednesday	Responding to God's Word	Receiving the Word of God
Thursday	Giving glory to God	Sharing in the work of the Church
Friday	Remembering Christ's Passion	Seeking God's forgiveness
Saturday	Looking for the coming of the kingdom	Discerning the presence of God

When you finish the fourteenth day, you can start again. However, you may prefer, at least at times, to choose a form on the basis of the theme rather than the day. For example, if you want to focus on the work of the Spirit, you will find the Monday forms particularly helpful. Equally, you will find certain days are especially appropriate for different seasons of the year. For example:

Sunday	Easter	Thursday	Epiphany
Monday	Pentecost	Friday	Lent
Tuesday	Advent	Saturday	All Saintstide
Wednesday	Christmas		

SUNDAY: Meeting the risen Christ

Preparing

I wait for the Lord; my soul waits for him;
in his word is my hope.

My soul waits for the Lord,
   more than the night watch for the morning,
more than the night watch for the morning.

Psalm 130. 4–5

Hearing

A reading about the risen Christ, from Luke 24. 28–35

As they came near the village to which they were going, he walked
ahead as if he were going on. But they urged him strongly, saying, 'Stay
with us, because it is almost evening and the day is now nearly over.' So
he went in to stay with them. When he was at the table with them, he
took bread, blessed and broke it, and gave it to them. Then their eyes
were opened, and they recognized him; and he vanished from their
sight. They said to each other, 'Were not our hearts burning within us
while he was talking to us on the road, while he was opening the scriptures to us?' That same hour they got up and returned to Jerusalem; and
they found the eleven and their companions gathered together. They
were saying, 'The Lord has risen indeed, and he has appeared to Simon!'
Then they told what had happened on the road, and how he had been
made known to them in the breaking of the bread.

Responding

*A time to reflect on the reading, to praise God and to pray (especially for
a readiness to meet with Christ), concluding with this Collect and the
Lord's Prayer.*

Almighty Father,
who in your great mercy gladdened the disciples
   with the sight of the risen Lord:
give us such knowledge of his presence with us,
that we may be strengthened and sustained
   by his risen life
and serve you continually in righteousness and truth;
through Jesus Christ your Son our Lord.

Third Sunday of Easter, CW

More material for prayer and praise

A hymn in praise of God's love

Love Divine, all loves excelling,
Joy of heaven, to earth come down,
Fix in us thy humble dwelling,
All thy faithful mercies crown.
Jesu, thou art all compassion,
Pure unbounded love thou art;
Visit us with thy salvation,
Enter every trembling heart.

Come, almighty to deliver,
Let us all thy life receive;
Suddenly return, and never,
Never more thy temples leave.
Thee we would be always blessing,
Serve thee as thy hosts above,
Pray, and praise thee, without ceasing,
Glory in thy perfect love.

Finish then thy new creation,
Pure and spotless let us be;
Let us see thy great salvation,
Perfectly restored in thee!
Changed from glory into glory,
Till in heaven we take our place,
Till we cast our crowns before thee,
Lost in wonder, love, and praise!
Charles Wesley, 1707–88 (NEH)

A prayer of grateful response

Father of all,
we give you thanks and praise,
that when we were still far off
you met us in your Son and brought us home.
Dying and living, he declared your love,
gave us grace, and opened the gate of glory.
May we who share Christ's body live his risen life;
we who drink his cup bring life to others;
we whom the Spirit lights give light to the world.
Keep us firm in the hope you have set before us,
so we and all your children shall be free,
and the whole earth live to praise your name;
through Christ our Lord.
From Holy Communion, Order One, CW

MONDAY: Celebrating God's work in creation

Preparing

You are worthy of our thanks and praise,
Lord God of truth,
for by the breath of your mouth
you have spoken your word,
and all things have come into being.
From Eucharistic Prayer F, CW

Hearing

A reading about the creation of the world and the responsibility of humanity, from Genesis 1. 26–31a

Then God said, 'Let us make humankind in our image, according to our likeness; and let them have dominion over the fish of the sea, and over the birds of the air, and over the cattle, and over all the wild animals of the earth, and over every creeping thing that creeps upon the earth.'

So God created humankind in his image,
in the image of God he created them;
male and female he created them.

God blessed them, and God said to them, 'Be fruitful and multiply, and fill the earth and subdue it; and have dominion over the fish of the sea and over the birds of the air and over every living thing that moves upon the earth.' God said, 'See, I have given you every plant yielding seed that is upon the face of all the earth, and every tree with seed in its fruit; you shall have them for food. And to every beast of the earth, and to every bird of the air, and to everything that creeps on the earth, everything that has the breath of life, I have given every green plant for food.' And it was so. God saw everything that he had made, and indeed, it was very good. And there was evening and there was morning, the sixth day.

Responding

A time to reflect on the reading, to praise God and to pray (especially for the care of the earth), concluding with this Collect and the Lord's Prayer.

Almighty God,
you have created the heavens and the earth
and made us in your own image:
teach us to discern your hand in all your works
and your likeness in all your children;
through Jesus Christ your Son our Lord,
who with you and the Holy Spirit
    reigns supreme over all things
now and for ever.
Second Sunday before Lent, CW

More material for prayer and praise

A psalm of praise to the Creator

O Lord our governor,
how glorious is your name in all the world!

Your majesty above the heavens is praised
out of the mouths of babes at the breast.

You have founded a stronghold against your foes,
that you might still the enemy and the avenger.

When I consider your heavens, the work of your fingers,
the moon and the stars that you have ordained,

What is man, that you should be mindful of him;
the son of man, that you should seek him out?

You have made him little lower than the angels
and crown him with glory and honour.

You have given him dominion over the works of your hands
and put all things under his feet,

All sheep and oxen,
even the wild beasts of the field,

The birds of the air, the fish of the sea
and whatsoever moves in the paths of the sea.

O Lord our governor,
how glorious is your name in all the world!

Glory . . .
Psalm 8

A prayer for the morning

Almighty and everlasting God,
we thank you that you have brought us safely
to the beginning of this day.
Keep us from falling into sin
or running into danger,
order us in all our doings
and guide us to do always
what is righteous in your sight;
through Jesus Christ our Lord.
CW

TUESDAY: Waiting for the coming of Christ

Preparing

Almighty God,
to whom all hearts are open,
all desires known,
and from whom no secrets are hidden:
cleanse the thoughts of our hearts
by the inspiration of your Holy Spirit,
that we may perfectly love you,
and worthily magnify your holy name;
through Christ our Lord.
The Collect for Purity, CW

Hearing

A reading about God's promise of salvation, from Isaiah 40. 1–5 (AV)

Comfort ye, comfort ye my people, saith your God. Speak ye comfort-
ably to Jerusalem, and cry unto her, that her warfare is accomplished,
that her iniquity is pardoned: for she hath received of the Lord's hand
double for all her sins. The voice of him that crieth in the wilderness,
'Prepare ye the way of the Lord, make straight in the desert a highway
for our God. Every valley shall be exalted, and every mountain and hill
shall be made low: and the crooked shall be made straight, and the
rough places plain. And the glory of the Lord shall be revealed, and all
flesh shall see it together: for the mouth of the Lord hath spoken it.'

Responding

*A time to reflect on the reading, to praise God and to pray (especially for
the suffering places of the world), concluding with this Collect and the
Lord's Prayer.*

Almighty God,
who alone can bring order
to the unruly wills and passions of sinful humanity:
give your people grace
so to love what you command
and to desire what you promise,
that, among the many changes of this world,
our hearts may surely there be fixed
where true joys are to be found;
through Jesus Christ your Son our Lord.
Third Sunday before Lent, CW

More material for prayer and praise

Zechariah's Song – Luke 1. 68–79

Blessed be the Lord the God of Israel,
who has come to his people and set them free.

He has raised up for us a mighty Saviour,
born of the house of his servant David.

Through his holy prophets God promised of old
to save us from our enemies,
   from the hands of all that hate us,

To show mercy to our ancestors,
and to remember his holy covenant.

This was the oath God swore to our father Abraham:
to set us free from the hands of our enemies,

Free to worship him without fear,
holy and righteous in his sight
   all the days of our life.

And you, child, shall be called the prophet of the Most High,
for you will go before the Lord to prepare his way,

To give his people knowledge of salvation
by the forgiveness of all their sins.

In the tender compassion of our God
the dawn from on high shall break upon us,

To shine on those who dwell in darkness and the
   shadow of death,
and to guide our feet into the way of peace.

Glory . . .
Benedictus, CW

A hymn of Christ's coming

Hail to the Lord's Anointed!
Great David's greater Son;
Hail, in the time appointed,
His reign on earth begun!
He comes to break oppression,
To set the captive free;
To take away transgression,
And rule in equity.
From a hymn by James Montgomery, 1771–1854 (NEH)

WEDNESDAY: Responding to God's word

Preparing

How wonderful the work of your hands, O Lord.
As a mother tenderly gathers her children,
you embraced a people as your own.
From them you raised up Jesus our Saviour, born of Mary,
to be the living bread,
in whom all our hungers are satisfied.
From Eucharistic Prayer G, CW

Hearing

A reading about Mary, Jesus' mother, from Luke 1. 26–38

In the sixth month the angel Gabriel was sent by God to a town in Galilee called Nazareth, to a virgin engaged to a man whose name was Joseph, of the house of David. The virgin's name was Mary. And he came to her and said, 'Greetings, favoured one! The Lord is with you.' But she was much perplexed by his words and pondered what sort of greeting this might be. The angel said to her, 'Do not be afraid, Mary, for you have found favour with God. And now, you will conceive in your womb and bear a son, and you will name him Jesus. He will be great, and will be called Son of the Most High, and the Lord God will give to him the throne of his ancestor David. He will reign over the house of Jacob for ever, and of his kingdom there will be no end.' Mary said to the angel, 'How can this be, since I am a virgin?' The angel said to her, 'The Holy Spirit will come upon you, and the power of the Most High will overshadow you; therefore the child to be born will be holy; he will be called Son of God. And now, your relative Elizabeth in her old age has also conceived a son; and this is the sixth month for her who was said to be barren. For nothing will be impossible with God.' Then Mary said, 'Here am I, the servant of the Lord; let it be with me according to your word.' Then the angel departed from her.

Responding

A time to reflect on the reading, to praise God and to pray (especially for those seeking faith in Christ), concluding with this Collect and the Lord's Prayer.

God our redeemer,
who prepared the Blessed Virgin Mary
to be the mother of your Son:
grant that, as she looked for his coming as our saviour,
so we may be ready to greet him
when he comes again as our judge . . .
Fourth Sunday of Advent, CW

More material for prayer and praise

Mary's Song of Praise – Luke 1. 46–55

My soul proclaims the greatness of the Lord,
    my spirit rejoices in God my Saviour;
he has looked with favour on his lowly servant.

From this day all generations will call me blessed;
the Almighty has done great things for me
    and holy is his name.

He has mercy on those who fear him,
from generation to generation.

He has shown strength with his arm
and has scattered the proud in their conceit,

Casting down the mighty from their thrones
and lifting up the lowly.

He has filled the hungry with good things
and sent the rich away empty.

He has come to the aid of his servant Israel,
to remember his promise of mercy,

The promise made to our ancestors,
to Abraham and his children for ever.

Glory . . .
Magnificat, CW

A prayer of self-offering to God

Teach me to serve thee as thou deservest;
To give and not to count the cost,
To fight and not to heed the wounds,
To toil and not to seek for rest,
To labour and not to seek for any reward,
Save that of knowing that I do thy will.
St Ignatius Loyola, 1491–1556

THURSDAY: Giving glory to God

Preparing

Alleluia.

O praise God in his holiness;
praise him in the firmament of his power.

Let everything that has breath
praise the Lord.
Alleluia.

Psalm 150. 1, 6

Hearing

A reading about the call of a prophet, from Isaiah 6. 1–8 (NIV)

In the year that King Uzziah died, I saw the Lord seated on a throne, high and exalted, and the train of his robe filled the temple. Above him were seraphs, each with six wings: With two wings they covered their faces, with two they covered their feet, and with two they were flying. And they were calling to one another:

'Holy, holy, holy is the Lord Almighty;
the whole earth is full of his glory.'

At the sound of their voices the doorposts and thresholds shook and the temple was filled with smoke. 'Woe to me!' I cried. 'I am ruined! For I am a man of unclean lips, and I live among a people of unclean lips, and my eyes have seen the King, the Lord Almighty.'

Then one of the seraphs flew to me with a live coal in his hand, which he had taken with tongs from the altar. With it he touched my mouth and said, 'See, this has touched your lips; your guilt is taken away and your sin atoned for.' Then I heard the voice of the Lord saying, 'Whom shall I send? And who will go for us?' And I said, 'Here am I; send me!'

Responding

A time to reflect on the reading, to praise God and to pray (especially for ears to hear God's call), concluding with this Collect and the Lord's Prayer.

Almighty God,
you have made us for yourself,
and our hearts are restless till they find their rest in you:
pour your love into our hearts and draw us to yourself,
and so bring us at last to your heavenly city
where we shall see you face to face;
through Jesus Christ your Son our Lord.

Seventeenth Sunday after Trinity, CW

More material for prayer and praise

A psalm of God's glory

The earth is the Lord's and all that fills it,
the compass of the world and all who dwell therein.

For he has founded it upon the seas
and set it firm upon the rivers of the deep.

'Who shall ascend the hill of the Lord,
or who can rise up in his holy place?'

'Those who have clean hands and a pure heart,
who have not lifted up their soul to an idol,
    nor sworn an oath to a lie;

'They shall receive a blessing from the Lord,
a just reward from the God of their salvation.'

Such is the company of those who seek him,
of those who seek your face, O God of Jacob.

Lift up your heads, O gates;
    be lifted up, you everlasting doors;
and the King of glory shall come in.

'Who is the King of glory?'
'The Lord, strong and mighty,
    the Lord who is mighty in battle.'

Lift up your heads, O gates;
    be lifted up, you everlasting doors;
and the King of glory shall come in.

'Who is this King of glory?'
'The Lord of hosts,
    he is the King of glory.'

Glory . . .
Psalm 24

Aaron's blessing

The Lord bless us and watch over us;
the Lord make his face shine upon us and be gracious to us;
the Lord look kindly on us and give us peace.
From Numbers 6. 24–6

FRIDAY: Remembering Christ's Passion

Preparing

Holy God,
holy and strong,
holy and immortal,
have mercy upon us.
From the Litany, CW

Hearing

A reading about the crucifixion, from Mark 15. 25–7, 33–9

It was nine o'clock in the morning when they crucified him. The inscription of the charge against him read, 'The King of the Jews.' And with him they crucified two bandits, one on his right and one on his left.

When it was noon, darkness came over the whole land until three in the afternoon. At three o'clock Jesus cried out with a loud voice, 'Eloi, Eloi, lema sabachthani?' which means, 'My God, my God, why have you forsaken me?' When some of the bystanders heard it, they said, 'Listen, he is calling for Elijah.' And someone ran, filled a sponge with sour wine, put it on a stick, and gave it to him to drink, saying, 'Wait, let us see whether Elijah will come to take him down.' Then Jesus gave a loud cry and breathed his last. And the curtain of the temple was torn in two, from top to bottom. Now when the centurion, who stood facing him, saw that in this way he breathed his last, he said, 'Truly this man was God's Son!'

Responding

A time to reflect on the reading, to praise God and to pray (especially for all who suffer), concluding with this Collect and the Lord's Prayer.

Most merciful God,
who by the death and resurrection of your Son Jesus Christ
delivered and saved the world:
grant that by faith in him who suffered on the cross
we may triumph in the power of his victory;
through Jesus Christ your Son our Lord,
who is alive and reigns with you,
in the unity of the Holy Spirit,
one God, now and for ever.
Fifth Sunday of Lent, CW

More material for prayer and praise

A hymn of Christ's self-giving

When I survey the wondrous Cross,
On which the Prince of glory died,
My richest gain I count but loss,
And pour contempt on all my pride.

Forbid it, Lord, that I should boast
Save in the death of Christ my God;
All the vain things that charm me most,
I sacrifice them to his blood.

See from his head, his hands, his feet,
Sorrow and love flow mingled down;
Did e'er such love and sorrow meet,
Or thorns compose so rich a crown?

Were the whole realm of nature mine,
That were an offering far too small;
Love so amazing, so divine,
Demands my life, my soul, my all.
Isaac Watts, 1674–1748 (HAM)

A prayer of thanks

Lord Jesus Christ, we thank you
for all the benefits you have won for us,
for all the pains and insults you have borne for us.
Most merciful redeemer,
friend and brother,
may we know you more clearly,
love you more dearly,
and follow you more nearly,
day by day.
St Richard of Chichester, 1197–1253

SATURDAY: Looking for the coming of the kingdom

Preparing

How lovely is your dwelling place, O Lord of hosts!
Psalm 84. 1a

Hearing

A reading about God's coming, from Revelation 21. 1–7

Then I saw a new heaven and a new earth; for the first heaven and the first earth had passed away, and the sea was no more. And I saw the holy city, the new Jerusalem, coming down out of heaven from God, prepared as a bride adorned for her husband. And I heard a loud voice from the throne saying,

'See, the home of God is among mortals.
He will dwell with them
they will be his peoples,
and God himself will be with them;
he will wipe every tear from their eyes.
Death will be no more;
mourning and crying and pain will be no more,
for the first things have passed away.'

And the one who was seated on the throne said, 'See, I am making all things new.' Also he said, 'Write this, for these words are trustworthy and true.' Then he said to me, 'It is done! I am the Alpha and the Omega; the beginning and the end. To the thirsty I will give water as a gift from the spring of the water of life. Those who conquer will inherit these things, and I will be their God and they will be my children.'

Responding

A time to reflect on the reading, to praise God and to pray (especially for all who work for the coming of God's kingdom), concluding with this Collect and the Lord's Prayer.

Almighty Father,
whose will is to restore all things
in your beloved Son, the King of all:
govern the hearts and minds of those in authority,
and bring the families of the nations,
divided and torn apart by the ravages of sin,
to be subject to his just and gentle rule . . .
Third Sunday before Advent, CW

More material for prayer and praise

Simeon's Song – Luke 2. 29–32

Lord, now lettest thou thy servant depart in peace:
according to thy word.

For mine eyes have seen:
thy salvation;

Which thou hast prepared:
before the face of all people;

To be a light to lighten the Gentiles:
and to be the glory of thy people Israel.

Glory . . .
Nunc dimittis, BCP and CW

A song to the Saviour from Holy Communion, CW

Jesus, Lamb of God,
have mercy on us.

Jesus, bearer of our sins,
have mercy on us.

Jesus, redeemer of the world,
grant us peace.
Agnus Dei

A prayer for the coming of God's Spirit, from Night Prayer (Compline), CCP

Come, O Spirit of God,
and make within us your dwelling place and home.
May our darkness be dispelled by your light,
and our troubles calmed by your peace;
may all evil be redeemed by your love,
all pain transformed through the suffering of Christ,
and all dying glorified in his risen life.

SUNDAY: Worshipping God in the risen Christ

Preparing

Come, let us worship and bow down
and kneel before the Lord our Maker.

From Venite, a Song of Triumph, Psalm 95. 6

Hearing

A reading about the privilege of worship, from Hebrews 4. 14–16

Since, then, we have a great high priest who has passed through the
heavens, Jesus, the Son of God, let us hold fast to our confession. For
we do not have a high priest who is unable to sympathize with our
weaknesses, but we have one who in every respect has been tested as we
are, yet without sin. Let us therefore approach the throne of grace with
boldness, so that we may receive mercy and find grace to help in time
of need.

Responding

*A time to reflect on the reading, to praise God and to pray (especially for
those who lead God's people), concluding with this Collect and the Lord's
Prayer.*

Almighty God,
who built your Church upon the foundation
    of the apostles and prophets,
with Jesus Christ himself as the chief cornerstone:
so join us together in unity of spirit by their doctrine,
that we may be made a holy temple acceptable to you;
through Jesus Christ your Son our Lord,
who is alive and reigns with you,
in the unity of the Holy Spirit,
one God, now and for ever.

St Simon and St Jude, CW

More material for prayer and praise

A hymn of confidence

No condemnation now I dread;
Jesus, and all in Him, is mine!
Alive in Him, my living Head,
And clothed in righteousness divine,
Bold I approach the eternal throne,
and claim the crown, through Christ my own.
From 'And can it be' by Charles Wesley, 1707–88

A prayer of thanks

Almighty God, Father of all mercies,
we thine unworthy servants
    do give thee most humble and hearty thanks
for all thy goodness and loving-kindness to us and to all men;
We bless thee for our creation, preservation,
    and all the blessings of this life;
but above all for thine inestimable love
in the redemption of the world by our Lord Jesus Christ,
for the means of grace, and for the hope of glory.
And we beseech thee, give us that due sense of all thy mercies,
that our hearts may be unfeignedly thankful,
and that we shew forth thy praise, not only with our lips,
    but in our lives;
by giving up ourselves to thy service,
and by walking before thee in holiness and righteousness
    all our days;
through Jesus Christ our Lord,
to whom with thee and the Holy Ghost
be all honour and glory, world without end.
The General Thanksgiving, BCP and CW

A song of obedience

Many are the words we speak,
many are the songs we sing;
many kinds of offering,
but now to live the life.
From 'Now to Live the Life' by Matt Redman, 1974

MONDAY: Receiving God's life through the Spirit

Preparing

Renew us by your Spirit,
inspire us with your love
and unite us in the body of your Son,
Jesus Christ our Lord.
From Eucharistic Prayer A, CW

Hearing

A reading about the work of the Spirit, from Romans 8. 14–17, 22–7

For all who are led by the Spirit of God are children of God. For you did not receive a spirit of slavery to fall back into fear, but you have received a spirit of adoption. When we cry, 'Abba! Father!' it is that very Spirit bearing witness with our spirit that we are children of God, and if children, then heirs, heirs of God and joint heirs with Christ – if, in fact, we suffer with him so that we may also be glorified with him.

We know that the whole creation has been groaning in labour pains until now; and not only the creation, but we ourselves, who have the first fruits of the Spirit, groan inwardly while we wait for adoption, the redemption of our bodies. For in hope we were saved. Now hope that is seen is not hope. For who hopes for what is seen? But if we hope for what we do not see, we wait for it with patience.

Likewise the Spirit helps us in our weakness; for we do not know how to pray as we ought, but that very Spirit intercedes with sighs too deep for words. And God, who searches the heart, knows what is in the mind of the Spirit, because the Spirit intercedes for the saints according to the will of God.

Responding

A time to reflect on the reading, to praise God and to pray (especially for the work of the Spirit), concluding with this Collect and the Lord's Prayer.

O God, forasmuch as without you
we are not able to please you;
mercifully grant that your Holy Spirit
may in all things direct and rule our hearts;
through Jesus Christ your Son our Lord.
Nineteenth Sunday after Trinity, CW

More material for prayer and praise

A psalm of trust in God's help

I lift up my eyes to the hills;
from where is my help to come?

My help comes from the Lord,
the maker of heaven and earth.

He will not suffer your foot to stumble;
he who watches over you will not sleep.

Behold, he who keeps watch over Israel
shall neither slumber nor sleep.

The Lord himself watches over you;
the Lord is your shade at your right hand,

So that the sun shall not strike you by day,
neither the moon by night.

The Lord shall keep you from all evil;
it is he who shall keep your soul.

The Lord shall keep watch over your going out
    and your coming in,
from this time forth for evermore.

Glory . . .
Psalm 121

A hymn for the work of the Spirit

Come, Holy Ghost, our souls inspire,
And lighten with celestial fire;
Thou the anointing Spirit art,
Who dost thy sevenfold gifts impart.

Thy blessed unction from above
Is comfort, life and fire of love;
Enable with perpetual light
The dullness of our blinded sight.

Teach us to know the Father, Son,
And thee, of Both, to be but One;
That through the ages all along
This may be our endless song:

Praise to thy eternal merit,
Father, Son and Holy Spirit.
Amen.
Veni creator Spiritus, CW

TUESDAY: Welcoming the light of Christ

Preparing

The Lord is my light and my salvation;
    whom shall I fear?
The Lord is the strength of my life;
    of whom then shall I be afraid?
Psalm 27. 1

Hearing

A reading about God's light in Christ, from John 3. 16–21

'For God so loved the world that he gave his only Son, so that everyone who believes in him may not perish but may have eternal life.

'Indeed, God did not send the Son into the world to condemn the world, but in order that the world might be saved through him. Those who believe in him are not condemned; but those who do not believe are condemned already, because they have not believed in the name of the only Son of God. And this is the judgement, that the light has come into the world, and people loved darkness rather than light because their deeds were evil. For all who do evil hate the light and do not come to the light, so that their deeds may not be exposed. But those who do what is true come to the light, so that it may be clearly seen that their deeds have been done in God.'

Responding

A time to reflect on the reading, to praise God and to pray (especially for leaders of the nations), concluding with this Collect and the Lord's Prayer.

Almighty God,
give us grace to cast away the works of darkness
and to put on the armour of light,
now in the time of this mortal life,
in which your Son Jesus Christ
    came to us in great humility;
that on the last day,
when he shall come again in his glorious majesty
    to judge the living and the dead,
we may rise to the life immortal;
through him who is alive and reigns
with you in the unity of the Holy Spirit,
one God, now and for ever.
First Sunday of Advent, CW

More material for prayer and praise

A psalm of praise

Alleluia.
Praise the Lord, O my soul:
while I live will I praise the Lord;
as long as I have any being,
I will sing praises to my God.

Put not your trust in princes,
nor in any human power,
for there is no help in them.

When their breath goes forth, they return to the earth;
on that day all their thoughts perish.

Happy are those who have the God of Jacob for their help,
whose hope is in the Lord their God;

Who made heaven and earth,
the sea and all that is in them;
who keeps his promise for ever;

Who gives justice to those that suffer wrong
and bread to those who hunger.

The Lord looses those that are bound;
the Lord opens the eyes of the blind;

The Lord lifts up those who are bowed down;
the Lord loves the righteous;

The Lord watches over the stranger in the land;
he upholds the orphan and widow;
but the way of the wicked he turns upside down.

The Lord shall reign for ever,
your God, O Zion, throughout all generations.
Alleluia.

Glory . . .
Psalm 146

A prayer for God's protection

Lighten our darkness, we beseech thee, O Lord;
and by thy great mercy defend us
from all perils and dangers of this night;
for the love of thy only Son, our Saviour, Jesus Christ.
From Evening Prayer, BCP and CW

WEDNESDAY: Receiving the Word of God

Preparing

Holy, holy, holy Lord,
God of power and might,
heaven and earth are full of your glory.
Hosanna in the highest.

Blessed is he who comes in the name of the Lord.
Hosanna in the highest.
Sanctus and Benedictus from the Eucharistic Prayer, CW

Hearing

A reading about the Word of God, from John 1. 1–5, 14–18

In the beginning was the Word, and the Word was with God, and the Word was God. He was in the beginning with God. All things came into being through him, and without him not one thing came into being. What has come into being in him was life, and the life was the light of all people. The light shines in the darkness, and the darkness did not overcome it.

And the Word became flesh and lived among us, and we have seen his glory, the glory as of a father's only son, full of grace and truth. (John testified to him and cried out, 'This was he of whom I said, "He who comes after me ranks ahead of me because he was before me."') From his fullness we have all received, grace upon grace. The law indeed was given through Moses; grace and truth came through Jesus Christ. No one has ever seen God. It is God the only Son, who is close to the Father's heart, who has made him known.

Responding

A time to reflect on the reading, to praise God and to pray (especially for God's Word to be made known), concluding with this Collect and the Lord's Prayer.

Almighty God,
in Christ you make all things new:
transform the poverty of our nature
   by the riches of your grace,
and in the renewal of our lives
make known your heavenly glory;
through Jesus Christ your Son our Lord.
Second Sunday of Epiphany, CW

More material for prayer and praise
The Gloria

Glory be to God on high,
and in earth peace, good will towards men.

We praise thee, we bless thee,
we worship thee, we glorify thee,
we give thanks to thee for thy great glory,
O Lord God, heavenly King,
God the Father almighty.

O Lord, the only-begotten Son Jesu Christ;
O Lord God, Lamb of God, Son of the Father,
that takest away the sins of the world,
have mercy upon us.
Thou that takest away the sins of the world,
have mercy upon us.
Thou that takest away the sins of the world,
receive our prayer.
Thou that sittest at the right hand of God the Father,
have mercy upon us.

For thou only art holy;
thou only art the Lord;
thou only, O Christ,
with the Holy Ghost,
art most high
in the glory of God the Father.
Amen.
From Holy Communion, BCP and CW

A confession of faith in Christ

We believe in one Lord, Jesus Christ,
the only Son of God,
eternally begotten of the Father,
God from God, Light from Light,
true God from true God.
From the Nicene Creed

Scots Celtic blessing

Deep peace of the running wave to you,
Deep peace of the flowing air to you,
Deep peace of the quiet earth to you,
Deep peace of the shining stars to you,
Deep peace of the Son of Peace to you.

THURSDAY: Sharing in the work of the Church

Preparing

The glorious company of apostles praise you.
The noble fellowship of prophets praise you.
The white-robed army of martyrs praise you.
Throughout the world the holy Church acclaims you:
Father, of majesty unbounded,
your true and only Son, worthy of all praise,
the Holy Spirit, advocate and guide.

From Te Deum Laudamus, CW

Hearing

A reading about Jesus commissioning the disciples, from Matthew 28.16–20

Now the eleven disciples went to Galilee, to the mountain to which Jesus had directed them. When they saw him, they worshipped him; but some doubted. And Jesus came and said to them, 'All authority in heaven and on earth has been given to me. Go therefore and make disciples of all nations, baptizing them in the name of the Father and of the Son and of the Holy Spirit, and teaching them to obey everything that I have commanded you. And remember, I am with you always, to the end of the age.'

Responding

A time to reflect on the reading, to praise God and to pray (especially for the will to serve God), concluding with this Collect and the Lord's Prayer.

Almighty God,
by whose grace alone we are accepted
    and called to your service:
strengthen us by your Holy Spirit
and make us worthy of our calling;
through Jesus Christ your Son our Lord.

Fifth Sunday before Lent, CW

More material for prayer and praise

A song of joy – Psalm 100

O be joyful in the Lord, all the earth;
serve the Lord with gladness
   and come before his presence with a song.

Know that the Lord is God;
it is he that has made us and we are his;
   we are his people and the sheep of his pasture.

Enter his gates with thanksgiving
   and his courts with praise;
give thanks to him and bless his name.

For the Lord is gracious; his steadfast love is everlasting,
and his faithfulness endures from generation to generation.

Glory . . .
Jubilate, CW

A prayer of affirmation

I believe that you created me:
let not the work of your hands be despised.

I believe that I am after your image and likeness:
let not your own likeness be defaced.

I believe that you saved me by your blood:
let not the price of the ransom be squandered.

I believe that you proclaimed me a Christian in your name:
let not your namesake be scorned.

I believe that you hallowed me in rebirth:
let not that consecration be despoiled.

I believe that you engrafted me into the cultivated olive-tree:
let not the limb of your mystical body be cut out.
Lancelot Andrewes, 1555–1626 (trans. Stevenson and Bradley)

A prayer of intercession

Look with favour on your people
and in your mercy hear the cry of our hearts.
Bless the earth,
heal the sick,
let the oppressed go free
and fill your Church with power from on high.
From Eucharistic Prayer F, CW

FRIDAY: Seeking God's forgiveness

Preparing

Most merciful God,
Father of our Lord Jesus Christ,
we confess that we have sinned
in thought, word and deed.
We have not loved you with our whole heart.
We have not loved our neighbours as ourselves.
In your mercy
forgive what we have been,
help us to amend what we are,
and direct what we shall be;
that we may do justly,
love mercy,
and walk humbly with you, our God.
A Confession, CW

Hearing

A reading about the humility of Christ, from Philippians 2. 5–11

Let the same mind be in you that was in Christ Jesus, who, though he
was in the form of God, did not regard equality with God as something
to be exploited, but emptied himself, taking the form of a slave, being
born in human likeness. And being found in human form, he humbled
himself and became obedient to the point of death – even death on a
cross. Therefore God also highly exalted him and gave him the name
that is above every name, so that at the name of Jesus every knee should
bend, in heaven and on earth and under the earth, and every tongue
should confess that Jesus Christ is Lord, to the glory of God the Father.

Responding

*A time to reflect on the reading, to praise God and to pray (especially for
those imprisoned by sin), concluding with this Collect and the Lord's
Prayer.*

Almighty Father,
look with mercy on this your family
for which our Lord Jesus Christ was content to be betrayed
    and given up into the hands of sinners
    and to suffer death upon the cross;
who is alive and glorified with you and the Holy Spirit,
one God, now and for ever.
Good Friday, CW

More material for prayer and praise

A psalm of repentance

Have mercy on me, O God, in your great goodness;
according to the abundance of your compassion
   blot out my offences.

Wash me thoroughly from my wickedness
and cleanse me from my sin.

For I acknowledge my faults
and my sin is ever before me.

Against you only have I sinned
and done what is evil in your sight,

So that you are justified in your sentence
and righteous in your judgement.

Deliver me from my guilt, O God,
   the God of my salvation,
and my tongue shall sing of your righteousness.

O Lord, open my lips
and my mouth shall proclaim your praise.

For you desire no sacrifice, else I would give it;
you take no delight in burnt offerings.

The sacrifice of God is a broken spirit;
a broken and contrite heart, O God, you will not despise.

Glory . . .
Psalm 51. 1–6, 15–18

A prayer that we may love God

O Lord our God,
grant us grace to desire thee with our whole heart;
that so desiring thee we may seek and find thee,
and so finding thee we may love thee,
and loving thee may hate those sins
from which thou hast redeemed us;
through our Lord Jesus Christ.
St Anselm, 1033–1109

SATURDAY: Discerning the presence of God

Preparing

God be in my head, and in my understanding;
God be in my eyes, and in my looking;
God be in my mouth, and in my speaking;
God be in my heart, and in my thinking;
God be at my end, and at my departing.

From the Sarum Primer

Hearing

A reading about wisdom, from Job 28. 12–13, 23–8

'But where shall wisdom be found?
    And where is the place of understanding?
Mortals do not know the way to it,
    and it is not found in the land of the living.
The deep says "It is not in me,"
    and the sea says, "It is not with me."
It cannot be bought for gold,
    and silver cannot be weighed out as its price.

'God understands the way to it,
    and he knows its place.
For he looks to the ends of the earth,
    and sees everything under the heavens.
When he gave to the wind its weight,
    and apportioned out the waters by measure;
when he made a decree for the rain,
    and a way for the thunderbolt;
then he saw it and declared it;
    he established it, and searched it out.
And he said to humankind,
"Truly, the fear of the Lord, that is wisdom;
    and to depart from evil is understanding."'

Responding

*A time to reflect on the reading, to praise God and to pray,
concluding with this Collect and the Lord's Prayer.*

O Lord, from whom all good things come:
grant to us your humble servants,
that by your holy inspiration
we may think those things that are good,
and by your merciful guiding may perform the same;
through our Lord Jesus Christ.

Weekdays after Pentecost, CW

More material for prayer and praise

A psalm of trust

The Lord is my shepherd;
therefore can I lack nothing.

He makes me lie down in green pastures
and leads me beside still waters.

He shall refresh my soul
and guide me in the paths of righteousness
    for his name's sake.

Though I walk through the valley of the shadow of death,
    I will fear no evil;
for you are with me;
    your rod and your staff, they comfort me.

You spread a table before me
    in the presence of those who trouble me;
you have anointed my head with oil
    and my cup shall be full.

Surely goodness and loving mercy shall follow me
    all the days of my life,
and I will dwell in the house of the Lord for ever.

Glory . . .
Psalm 23

A prayer of preparation for Holy Communion

Most merciful Lord,
your love compels us to come in.
Our hands were unclean,
our hearts were unprepared;
we were not fit
even to eat the crumbs from under your table.
But you, Lord, are the God of our salvation,
and share your bread with sinners.
So cleanse and feed us
with the precious body and blood of your Son,
that he may live in us and we in him;
and that we, with the whole company of Christ,
may sit and eat in your kingdom.
A Prayer of Humble Access, CW

Alternative readings

Sunday: Meeting the risen Christ
Exodus 16. 10–18   Bread from heaven
John 20. 10–18   Jesus appears to Mary Magdalene

Monday: Celebrating God's work in creation
Deuteronomy 26. 1–11   The firstfruits of the land
Colossians 1. 15–20   The first-born of all creation

Tuesday: Waiting for the coming of Christ
Isaiah 42. 1–9   The servant of the Lord
Matthew 25. 1–13   Keeping watch

Wednesday: Responding to God's Word
Exodus 3. 1–10   The call of Moses
Luke 10. 29–37   The Good Samaritan

Thursday: Giving glory to God
2 Chronicles 5. 11–14   God's glory fills the temple
Revelation 5. 11–14   The worship of heaven

Friday: Remembering Christ's Passion
Isaiah 53. 1–6   The suffering servant
Luke 23. 32–43   The cross and the criminals

Saturday: Looking for the coming of the kingdom
Isaiah 65. 17–25   New heavens and a new earth
Matthew 13. 31–5   Mustard seed and yeast

Sunday: Worshipping God in the risen Christ

Micah 6. 6–8	The requirement of the Lord
John 4. 21–6	Worshipping God in spirit and truth

Monday: Receiving God's life through the Spirit

1 Samuel 16. 6–13	Samuel anoints David
Galatians 5. 16–26	Living by the Spirit

Tuesday: Welcoming the light of Christ

Isaiah 49. 1–6	A light for all people
Ephesians 5. 6–21	Living as children of light

Wednesday: Receiving the Word of God

Proverbs 4. 1–9	Embracing God's Word
Mark 10. 46–52	Blind Bartimaeus receives his sight

Thursday: Sharing in the work of the Church

Jeremiah 1. 4–9	The call of Jeremiah
Romans 12. 1–8	Living sacrifices

Friday: Seeking God's forgiveness

Joel 2. 12–14	Call to repentance
Acts 2. 36–41	Repentance and baptism

Saturday: Discerning the presence of God

Psalm 139. 1–17	God's abiding presence
Luke 7. 18–23	John's disciples question Jesus

A cycle of readings (or lections) such as this is known as a lectionary. Other lectionaries for use on a daily basis can be found in the *BCP* and *CW*, both of which are published in booklet form by SPCK. The Bible Reading Fellowship, Scripture Union and other organisations also provide daily lectionaries, together with notes on the readings. These should be available through your church bookstall and can be found in most Christian bookshops.

PART THREE

Changing scenes of life

Part Three: Changing scenes of life

This section consists of prayers, Bible passages, hymns, poems and other material about various features of human experience from birth to death.

You may want to read appropriate sections prayerfully at particular periods or turning points of your life. For example, at the birth of a child or some other creative new venture in life you might reflect on 'Beginnings'; at a baptism or confirmation 'New beginnings' might speak to you; on holiday 'Contentment' might be appropriate; if you are facing illness you might meditate on the section 'Pain'; when you meet people of other faiths you might find help from 'Encountering other traditions', and so on. Or you might use a particular section as a way of entering into the experience of someone very different from yourself: for example, a young person might ruminate about the section on 'Growing older'.

You could also use some of the material in groups or individually to supplement the daily prayers in Part Two, 'Prayer for today'.

Through all the changing scenes of life,
    In trouble and in joy,
The praises of my God shall still
    My heart and tongue employ.

Tate and Brady, 1696 (NEH)

For everything there is a season, and a time for every matter under heaven:

a time to be born, and a time to die;
a time to plant, and a time to pluck up what is planted;
a time to kill, and a time to heal;
a time to break down, and a time to build up;
a time to weep, and a time to laugh;
a time to mourn, and a time to dance . . .

Ecclesiastes 3. 1–4

Beginnings

Almighty God,
who wonderfully created us in your own image
and yet more wonderfully restored us
through your Son Jesus Christ:
grant that, as he came to share in our humanity,
so we may share the life of his divinity;
who is alive and reigns with you,
in the unity of the Holy Spirit,
one God, now and for ever.

Christmas 1, CW

In the beginning God created the heavens and the earth. The earth
was without form and void, and darkness was upon the face of the
deep; and the Spirit of God was moving over the face of the waters.
And God said, 'Let there be light'; and there was light.

Genesis 1. 1–3 (RSV)

Where were you when I laid the foundation of the earth? . . . On
what were its bases sunk, or who laid its cornerstone, when the
morning stars sang together, and all the sons of God shouted for
joy?

Job 38. 4, 6–7 (RSV)

And while they were there, the time came for Mary to be delivered.
And she gave birth to her first-born son and wrapped him in
swaddling cloths, and laid him in a manger, because there was no
place for them in the inn.

Luke 2. 6–7 (RSV)

How could the human race go to God if God had not come to us?
How should we free ourselves from our birth into death if we had
not been born again according to faith by a new birth generously
given by God, thanks to that which came about from the Virgin's
womb?

Irenaeus of Lyons, c. 130–c. 208 (Clément, 1993)

It was Mary's own prediction, 'From henceforth all generations shall call me blessed' (Luke 1. 48), but the obligation is ours to call her, to esteem her so. If Elizabeth cried out with so 'loud a voice, Blessed art thou among women' (verse 42), when Christ was but newly conceived in her womb, what expressions of honour and admiration can we think sufficient, now that Christ is in heaven, and that mother with him? Far be it from any Christian to derogate from that special privilege granted her, which is incommunicable to any other. We cannot bear too reverend a regard unto the mother of our Lord, so long as we give her not that worship which is due unto the Lord himself. Let us keep the language of the primitive church: 'Let her be honoured and esteemed, let him be worshipped and adored.'

Bishop John Pearson, 1613–86

And then the Lord showed me more, a little thing, the size of a hazelnut, on the palm of my hand, round like a ball. I looked at it thoughtfully and wondered, 'What is this?' And the answer came, 'It is all that is made.' I marvelled that it continued to exist and did not suddenly disintegrate; it was so small. And again my mind supplied the answer, 'It exists, both now and for ever, because God loves it.' In short, everything owes its existence to the love of God. In this 'little thing' I saw three truths. The first is that God made it; the second is that God loves it; and the third is that God sustains it.

Julian of Norwich, 1342–1416

God is God. His first word to you, to me, is a word of permission. God does not want to be the whole universe. God does not want to be you or me ... God invites you to freedom: 'Let there be light.' ... A ten-year-old boy wrote, 'Yesterday I saw a robin let a worm go. That's like God.'

Angela Tilby, 1950–

'The kingdom of God is within you' (Luke 17. 21). The heart is a small vessel, but all things are contained in it; God is there, the angels are there, and there also is life and the Kingdom, the heavenly cities and the treasures of grace.

St Makarios, c. 300–90 (Ware, 1966)

Some people have a childhood so beautiful that it will not let their minds go, or so unsatisfactory that it breeds a hopeless longing for this crucial bit of the human joy they have been denied. Jesus never had the adventure and fulfilment of marriage and children, but the fact that he drew so much important imagery for the life of faith from the world of childhood suggests that the memory of his earliest days, graced with the beauty and love of one particular face, was part of the deep joy within his being.

Neville Ward, 1915–92

Teach me, my God and King,
   In all things thee to see;
And what I do in anything
   To do it as for thee!

A man that looks on glass,
   On it may stay his eye;
Or if he pleaseth, through it pass,
   And then the heaven espy.

George Herbert, 1593–1633 (NEH)

As it was, as it is, and as it shall be
Evermore, God of grace, God in Trinity!
With the ebb, with the flow, ever it is so,
God of grace, O Trinity, with the ebb and flow.

Celtic prayer (McLean, 1988)

New beginnings

Eternal Father,
who at the baptism of Jesus
revealed him to be your Son,
anointing him with the Holy Spirit:
grant to us, who are born again by water and the Spirit,
that we may be faithful to our calling as your adopted children;
through Jesus Christ your Son our Lord.

Baptism of Christ, CW

And when Jesus had been baptized, just as he came up from the water, suddenly the heavens were opened to him and he saw the Spirit of God descending like a dove and alighting on him. And a voice from heaven said, 'This is my Son, the Beloved, with whom I am well pleased.'

Matthew 3. 16–17

Nicodemus said to Jesus, 'How can anyone be born after having grown old? Can one enter a second time into the mother's womb and be born?' Jesus answered, 'Very truly, I tell you, no one can enter the kingdom of God without being born of water and Spirit.'

John 3. 4–5

In baptism, God calls us out of darkness into his marvellous light.
To follow Christ means dying to sin and rising to new life with him.
Therefore I ask:

Do you reject the devil and all rebellion against God?
I reject them.

Do you renounce the deceit and corruption of evil?
I renounce them.

Do you repent of the sins that separate us from God and neighbour?
I repent of them.

Do you turn to Christ as Saviour?
I turn to Christ.

Do you submit to Christ as Lord?
I submit to Christ.

Do you come to Christ, the way, the truth and the life?
I come to Christ.
From Holy Baptism, CW

May the cross of the Son of God,
which is mightier than all the hosts of Satan,
and more glorious than all the hosts of heaven,
abide with me in my going out and my coming in.
By day and by night, at morning and at evening,
at all times and in all places may it protect and defend me.
From the wrath of evildoers, from the assaults of evil spirits,
from foes visible and invisible, from the snares of the devil,
from all passions that beguile the soul and body:
may it guard, protect and deliver me.
An Indian prayer from Wholeness and Healing, CW

Joshua son of Nun was full of the spirit of wisdom, because Moses
had laid his hands on him.
Deuteronomy 34. 9

Confirmation is the ministry by which, through prayer with the
laying on of hands by the Bishop, the Holy Spirit is received to
complete what he began in Baptism, and to give strength for the
Christian life.
Revised Catechism

Defend, O Lord, your servants with your heavenly grace,
that they may continue yours for ever,
and daily increase in your Holy Spirit more and more,
until they come to your everlasting kingdom. Amen.
Confirmation Service, CW

O thou who camest from above,
    The pure celestial fire to impart,
Kindle a flame of sacred love
    On the mean altar of my heart.

There let it for thy glory burn
    With inextinguishable blaze,
And trembling to its source return
    In humble prayer, and fervent praise.

Charles Wesley, 1707–88 (NEH)

The approach of the Holy Spirit is gentle, his presence fragrant, his yoke very light; rays of light and knowledge shine forth before him as he comes. He comes with the heart of a true protector; he comes to save, to heal, to teach, to admonish, to strengthen, to console, to enlighten the mind, first of the man who receives him, then through him the minds of others also.

St Cyril of Jerusalem, 313–87 (Kenneth CGA, 1983)

Christian ran thus till he came at a place somewhat ascending; and upon that place stood a Cross, and a little below in the bottom, a sepulchre. So I saw in my dream, that just as Christian came up with the Cross, his burden loosed from off his shoulders, and fell from off his back; and began to tumble, and so continued to do till it came to the mouth of the sepulchre, where it fell in, and I saw it no more. Then was Christian glad and lightsome, and said with a merry heart, 'He hath given me rest, by his sorrow, and life, by his death.'

From Pilgrim's Progress *by John Bunyan, 1628–88*

God is with me now,
Closer than breathing,
And nearer than hands and feet.
God has made me for Himself.
I come from God,
I belong to God,
I go to God.
God knows me,
God loves me,
God has a use for me
Now and for ever.

Author unknown

I have learnt to love you late, Beauty at once so ancient and so new!
. . . You called me; you cried aloud to me; you broke my barrier of
deafness. You shone upon me; your radiance enveloped me; you
put my blindness to flight.

St Augustine, 354–430

The fire is salt, cleansing, healing, salutary. . . . May God give me
grace not to run from this fire, nor to throw away the cross; but
may he give me grace besides to recognise his handiwork in all men;
to acknowledge that converted or unconverted, he made them,
and filled them with all sorts of excellences. I must pray indeed for
men's conversion, but I must pray meanwhile for their happiness
and for their growth in mere humanity.

Austin Farrer, 1904–68

Be alive

Think freely: Practise patience:
Smile often: Savour special moments:
Live God's message: Make new
friends: Discover old ones: Tell those
you love that you do: Feel deeply:

Forget trouble: Forgive an enemy.
Pick some daisies: Share them: Keep
a promise: Look for rainbows: Gaze at
stars: See beauty everywhere: Work
hard: Be wise: Try to understand:
Take time for people: Make time for yourself.

Laugh heartily: Spread joy: Take a
chance: Reach out: Let someone in:
Try something new: Slow down: Be
soft sometimes: Celebrate life:
Believe in yourself: Trust others: See
a sunrise: Listen to rain: Reminisce:
Cry when you need to . . .

Author unknown

Choices

Almighty God,
you show to those who are in error the light of your truth,
that they may return to the way of righteousness:
grant to all those who are admitted
   into the fellowship of Christ's religion,
that they may reject those things
   that are contrary to their profession,
and follow all such things as are agreeable to the same;
through our Lord Jesus Christ.

Lent 2, CW

I call heaven and earth to witness against you today that I have set
before you life and death, blessings and curses. Choose life so that
you and your descendants may live, loving the Lord your God,
obeying him, and holding fast to him.

Deuteronomy 30. 19–20

And going a little farther, Jesus threw himself on the ground and
prayed that, if it were possible, the hour might pass from him. He
said 'Abba, Father, for you all things are possible; remove this cup
from me; yet, not what I want, but what you want.'

Mark 14. 35–6

Do not be conformed to this world, but be transformed by the
renewing of your minds, so that you may discern what is the will
of God – what is good and acceptable and perfect.

Romans 12. 2

On a huge hill,
Cragged, and steep, Truth stands, and he that will
Reach her, about must, and about must go.

John Donne, 1573–1631

Our deeds determine us as much as we determine our deeds. . . .
There is a terrible coercion in our deeds which may first turn the
honest man into a deceiver, and then reconcile him to the change.

From Adam Bede *by George Eliot, 1819–80*

Alas, poor Judas, we do not know by what degrees of falling away he slipped out of that kindness of Christ which it is life to have.

Austin Farrer, 1904–68

'It was necessary for the Christ to suffer'; but not because it had been laid down in a heavenly book or an earthly scripture, not because God desires suffering or insists on exacting it from a victim before he will forgive human beings their sins. It was necessary for the Christ to suffer because the character of the God ... is such that the way of the cross was in practice bound to be the way he would follow. Jesus did not come preaching the good news of the kingdom *in order* to get himself executed. ... He came to embody the love of God for his creation, accepting the consequences of doing so whatever these might be.

John Barton, 1948–

The Christian is not just to do certain things: he is to be a certain kind of person. It is enough to go through the outward motions of virtue, for it is the inmost state of the soul that matters in God's eyes.

Helen Oppenheimer, 1926–

Eternal Light, shine in our hearts,
Eternal Goodness, deliver us from evil,
Eternal Power, be our support,
Eternal Wisdom, scatter the darkness of our ignorance,
Eternal Pity, have mercy upon us;
that with all our heart and mind and soul and strength
we may seek thy face and be brought by thine
     infinite mercy
to thy holy presence; through Jesus Christ our Lord.

Alcuin of York, 735–804 (Milner-White and Briggs, 1959)

Father, hear the prayer we offer:
   Not for ease that prayer shall be,
But for strength that we may ever
   Live our lives courageously.

Maria Willis, 1824–1908 (NEH)

Work

Lord,
Take our hands and work with them;
Take our lips and speak through them;
Take our minds and think with them;
Take our hearts and set them on fire with love
for you and all creation.
Author unknown

All those rely on their hands, and each is skilful at his own craft.
Without them a city would have no inhabitants; no settlers or
travellers would come to it. Yet they are not in demand at public
discussions, nor do they attain to high office in the assembly. . . .
But they maintain the fabric of this world, and the practice of their
craft is their prayer.
Ecclesiasticus 38. 31–4 (REB)

Is not this the carpenter, the son of Mary?
Mark 6. 3

Paul went to see them, and, because he was of the same trade, he
stayed with them, and they worked together – by trade they were
tentmakers.
Acts 18. 2–3

Christian writings about work (especially other people's work) are
so often hopelessly pious or idealistic. . . . How can I serve God in
my work – as farmer, producer, manufacturer, technician, scientist,
administrator and so on? . . . The question, to which such men
want an answer, is what difference being a Christian makes to the
things that they do and the decisions that they make during the
working day.
Mark Gibbs, 1920–86, and Ralph Morton, 1900–77

Imagine the experience of coming home on Friday afternoon. The
week has flown by in a rush of activity. You are exhausted. And

there, in all its simplicity and splendour, is the Sabbath table: candles radiating the light that symbolises *shalom bayit*, peace in the home; wine, representing blessing and joy; and the two loaves of bread, recalling the double portion of manna that fell for the Israelites in the wilderness so that they would not have to gather food on the seventh day. Seeing that table you know that until tomorrow evening you will step into another world, one where there are no pressures to work or compete, no distractions or interruptions, just time to be together with family and friends . . . We can sometimes work so hard that we forget why we work at all. We don't live in order to labour. We labour in order to live. And the Sabbath is the day we stand still and just live, and let all the blessings we have accumulated catch up with us. The Sabbath was and remains a revolutionary idea. Many ancient religions had their holy days. But none had a day on which it was forbidden to work.

Jonathan Sacks, Chief Rabbi, 1948–

> Seed we bring
> **Lord, to thee, wilt thou bless them, O Lord!**
> Gardens we bring
> **Lord, to thee, wilt thou bless them, O Lord!**
> Hoes we bring
> **Lord, to thee, wilt thou bless them, O Lord!**
> Knives we bring
> **Lord, to thee, wilt thou bless them, O Lord!**
> Hands we bring
> **Lord, to thee, wilt thou bless them, O Lord!**
> Ourselves we bring
> **Lord, to thee, wilt thou bless them, O Lord!**
>
> *East African hymn used at a service for blessing of seeds*
> *(Appleton, 1985)*

God, in all that is most living and incarnate in Him, is not far away from us, altogether apart from the world we see, touch, hear, smell and taste about us. Rather He awaits us every instant in our action, in the work of the moment. There is a sense in which He is at the tip of my pen, my spade, my brush, my needle – of my heart and of my thought.

Pierre Teilhard de Chardin SJ, 1881–1955

Christians and many others . . . would insist that every man and woman has capabilities of some kind and that in our society all adults are citizens. As citizens each of them has a *duty* to contribute to the whole community by undertaking a share of the work to be done and that they also have the reverse of that duty, namely, the *right* to take their part in and to feel themselves to be part of the *working community*. It is for this reason that designed long-term unemployment will not be tolerated. It is immoral.

Church of England Board for Social Responsibility, 1969

Christ has no body now on earth but yours,
no hands but yours, no feet but yours;
yours are the eyes through which is to look out
Christ's compassion to the world,
yours are the feet with which he is to go about doing good,
and yours are the hands with which he is to bless us now.

St Teresa of Avila, 1515–82 (Herbert, 1993)

Love

To God the Father, who loved us, and made us accepted
    in the Beloved:
To God the Son, who loved us, and washed us from our
    sins in his own blood:
To God the Holy Spirit, who sheds the love of God
    abroad in our hearts.
To the one true God be all love and all glory, for time and
    for eternity.

Bishop Thomas Ken, 1637–1711 (Silk, 1986)

Set me as a seal upon your heart, as a seal upon your
    arm;
for love is strong as death, passion fierce as the grave.
Its flashes are flashes of fire, a raging flame.
Many waters cannot quench love, neither can floods
    drown it.

Song of Solomon 8. 6–7

For I am convinced that neither death, nor life, nor angels, nor
rulers, nor things present, nor things to come, nor powers, nor
height, nor depth, nor anything else in all creation, will be able to
separate us from the love of God in Christ Jesus our Lord.

Romans 8. 38–9

Beloved, let us love one another, because love is from God; everyone who loves is born of God and knows God. . . . We love because
he first loved us. Those who say 'I love God', and hate their brothers
or sisters, are liars; for those who do not love a brother or sister
whom they have seen, cannot love God whom they have not seen.

1 John 4. 7, 19–20

Blessed are those who love you, O God, and love their friends in
you and their enemies for your sake. They alone will never lose
those who are dear to them, for they love them in one who is never
lost, in God.

St Augustine, 354–430

To love at all is to be vulnerable. Love anything, and your heart will certainly be wrung and possibly be broken. If you want to make sure of keeping it intact, you must give your heart to no one, not even to an animal. Wrap it carefully round with hobbies and little luxuries; avoid all entanglements; lock it up safe in the casket or coffin of your selfishness. But in that casket – safe, dark, motionless, airless – it will change. It will not be broken; it will become unbreakable, impenetrable, irredeemable.... I believe that the most lawless and inordinate loves are less contrary to God's will than a self-invited and self-protective lovelessness.

C. S. Lewis, 1898–1963

My song is love unknown,
　My Saviour's love to me,
Love to the loveless shown,
　That they might lovely be.
　　O, who am I,
　　That for my sake
　　My Lord should take
　　Frail flesh, and die?

Samuel Crossman, 1624–83 (NEH)

Dearly beloved, we are gathered here in the sight of God and in the face of this congregation, to join together this man and this woman in Holy Matrimony; which is an honourable estate, instituted of God himself, signifying unto us the mystical union that is betwixt Christ and his Church; which holy estate Christ adorned and beautified with his presence, and first miracle that he wrought, in Cana of Galilee, and is commended in Holy Writ to be honourable among all men; and therefore is not by any to be enterprised, nor taken in hand, unadvisedly, lightly, or wantonly; but reverently, discreetly, soberly, and in the fear of God, duly considering the causes for which Matrimony was ordained.

Marriage Service, Series 1

I give you this ring
as a sign of our marriage.
With my body I honour you,
all that I am I give to you,
and all that I have I share with you,
within the love of God,
Father, Son and Holy Spirit.

Marriage Service, CW

And you held me

and you held me and there were no words
and there was no time and you held me
and there was only wanting and
being held and being filled with wanting
and I was nothing but letting go
and being held
and there were no words and there
needed to be no words
and there was no terror   only stillness
and I was wanting nothing and
it was fullness and it was like aching for God
and it was touch and warmth and
darkness and no time and no words and we flowed
and I flowed and I was not empty
and I was given up to the dark and
in the darkness I was not lost
and the wanting was like fullness and I could
hardly hold it and I was held and
you were dark and warm and without time and
without words and you held me

Janet Morley, 1951–

As a young mother, looking with disbelief, incredulity and shock upon the still-born face of my first daughter, I would have said a baby was misery and mystery.

Later on, lying in hospital, with my second, perfect girl in my arms, not quite choirs of angels, but nurses in capes carolling by lantern-light around our bed, a baby was joy, triumph, fulfilment. I was not to know then that it also meant years of lasting love.

Learning that the three-pound scrap of life in the incubator was my third, invalid daughter, meant a baby was a disaster. The six months of her life were a rage of grief, betrayal, rebellion and pure pain. Her death was part relief, part regret, wholly devastating.

I never saw a baby with my heart after that, so the first sight of my new-born grandson caught me unawares. My first impulse was to kneel. I would have said then that a baby was a small touch from the hand of God.

Now with another happy, laughing grandson to love, a baby is – what? Hope, perhaps, or promises? Or reassurances that there is some reason in the scheme of things.

What is a baby? It is Life, of course. What else?

Frances Mary Marston (Guinness, 1993)

Almighty God, like a loving parent gazing on his or her child, contemplates me in love . . . like the father I once watched on a beach. His child had just begun to walk. . . . With obvious delight it zigzagged drunkenly from the sea to the sand and back again, unaware that its father was looking on with equal delight, amusement and awe.

Joyce Huggett, 1937–

Walking away – for Sean

It is eighteen years ago, almost to the day –
A sunny day with the leaves just turning,
The touch-lines new-ruled – since I watched you play
Your first game of football, then, like a satellite
Wrenched from its orbit, go drifting away

Behind a scatter of boys. I can see
You walking away from me towards the school

With the pathos of a half-fledged thing set free
Into a wilderness, the gait of one
Who finds no path where the path should be.

That hesitant figure, eddying away
Like a winged seed loosened from its parent stem,
Has something I never quite grasp to convey
About nature's give-and-take – the small, the scorching
Ordeals which fire one's irresolute clay.

I have had worse partings, but none that so
Gnaws at my mind still. Perhaps it is roughly
Saying what God alone could perfectly show –
How selfhood begins with a walking away,
And love is proved in the letting go.
C. Day Lewis, 1904–72

God is as really our Mother as he is our Father.
Julian of Norwich, 1342–1416

I strolled with a friend outside Salisbury Cathedral. My friend
drew my attention to the tall, thin figure of a woman striding
purposefully away. . . . I wanted to meet this stranger, to walk with
her, talk with her. . . . But it was foolish to the point of absurdity.
For she was only a sculpture, a bronze statue of the Virgin Mary,
immobilized on a solid plinth. . . . She is definitely middle-aged.
And she is alone. Is *this* what draws me to her, I wonder? I too am
forty-something, single, and sometimes hate both. . . . This 'Mary'
would understand such feelings, I believe, for she has seen her
pearl taken away from before her eyes, that pearl of great price, her
firstborn son. And every line of her no longer youthful body
speaks of the pain of that loss. . . .

Thank you, Lord, that in the middle years of my present single-
ness I walk with you and your blessed mother in an ever-increasing
appreciation of the riches to be found and the gains to be won,
through loss.
Sue Rossetter, 1946– (Guinness, 1993)

Contentment

Be blessed, O God,
   in your doing, and your refraining,
   in your creating, and your sustaining,
   in your working, and in your rest.
   Quiet at the centre of movement,
   Joy at the centre of pain.
   Peace at the centre of strife.

Margaret Cropper, 1886–1980

God saw everything that he had made, and indeed, it was very good. . . . And on the seventh day God finished the work that he had done, and he rested.

Genesis 1. 31; 2.2

Thus says the Lord of hosts: Old men and old women shall again sit in the streets of Jerusalem, each with staff in hand because of their great age. And the streets of the city shall be full of boys and girls playing in its streets.

Zechariah 8. 4–5

I have learned to be content with whatever I have. I know what it is to have little, and I know what it is to have plenty.

Philippians 4. 11–12

The God of Genesis . . . stands back from what has been made and takes a break. God rests. God enjoys. And God makes it a rule of the busy universe that rest and passivity should be built in as the most essential part of the timetable.

Angela Tilby, 1950–

Moments of great calm,
Kneeling before an altar
Of wood in a stone church
In summer, waiting for the God
To speak; the air a staircase
For silence . . .

R. S. Thomas, 1913–2000

The glory of God is a living person and the life of humanity is the vision of God.

Irenaeus of Lyons, c. 130–c. 208 (Clément, 1993)

If you are a theologian you will pray truly; and if you pray truly you are a theologian.

Evagrius of Pontus, 346–99 (Clément, 1993)

How sweet the moonlight sleeps upon this bank!
Here will we sit and let the sounds of music
Creep in our ears: soft stillness and the night
Become the touches of sweet harmony.

From The Merchant of Venice *by William Shakespeare, 1564–1616*

Before prayer

I weave a silence on to my lips
I weave a silence into my mind
I weave a silence within my heart
I close my ears to distractions
I close my eyes to attractions
I close my heart to temptations

Calm me O Lord as you stilled the storm
Still me O Lord, keep me from harm
Let all tumult within me cease
Enfold me Lord in your peace

David Adam, 1936–

You say grace before meals.
All right.
But I say grace before the play and the opera,
And grace before the concert and pantomime,
And grace before I open a book,
And grace before sketching, painting,
Swimming, fencing, boxing, walking, playing, dancing,
And grace before I dip the pen in the ink.

G. K. Chesterton, 1874–1936 (Mackey, 1994)

On the Delectable Mountains of laughter we sense the glory which shall be revealed in us. . . . And although we are still on our journey, when we laugh we know that really we have already arrived. The party has begun and we are there.

Harry Williams CR, 1919–

I used to fight my devils in prayer, but now I send them up in jokes.

Rabbi Lionel Blue, 1930–

Praise, my soul, the King of heaven;
    To his feet thy tribute bring.
Ransomed, healed, restored, forgiven,
    Who like me his praise should sing?

H. F. Lyte, 1793–1847 (NEH)

God, give us grace
to accept with serenity the things that cannot be changed,
courage to change the things that should be changed,
and the wisdom to distinguish the one from the other.

Reinhold Niebuhr, 1892–1971

Sharing creation

Eternal God,
you crown the year with your goodness
and you give us the fruits of the earth in their season:
grant that we may use them to your glory,
for the relief of those in need and for our own well-being;
through Jesus Christ your Son our Lord,
who is alive and reigns with you,
in the unity of the Holy Spirit,
one God, now and for ever.

Harvest Thanksgiving, CW

God said, 'This is the sign of the covenant that I make between me
and you and every living creature that is with you, for all future
generations: I have set my bow in the clouds, and it shall be a sign
of the covenant between me and the earth.'

Genesis 9. 12–13

O all ye Works of the Lord, bless ye the Lord:
praise him and magnify him for ever.

O ye Angels of the Lord, bless ye the Lord;
O ye Heavens bless ye the Lord.
O ye Waters that be above the Firmament,
    bless ye the Lord;
O all ye Powers of the Lord, bless ye the Lord.
O ye Sun and Moon, bless ye the Lord;
O ye Stars of Heaven, bless ye the Lord.
O ye Showers and Dew, bless ye the Lord;
O ye Winds of God, bless ye the Lord.
O ye Fire and Heat, bless ye the Lord;
O ye Winter and Summer, bless ye the Lord.
O ye Dews and Frosts, bless ye the Lord;
O ye Frost and Cold, bless ye the Lord.
O ye Ice and Snow, bless ye the Lord;
O ye Nights and Days, bless ye the Lord.

O ye Light and Darkness, bless ye the Lord;
O ye Lightnings and Clouds, bless ye the Lord.

O let the Earth bless the Lord:
yea, let it praise him, and magnify him for ever.

From the Benedicite, BCP and CW

'Look at the birds of the air; they neither sow nor reap nor gather into barns, and yet your heavenly Father feeds them. . . . Consider the lilies of the field, how they grow; they neither toil nor spin, yet I tell you, even Solomon in all his glory was not clothed like one of these.'

Matthew 6. 26, 28–9

Praised be my Lord God with all his creatures, and
    especially our brother the sun . . .
Praised be my Lord for our sister the moon and for the
    stars . . .
Praised be my Lord for our sister water . . .
Praised be my Lord for our brother fire . . .
Praised be my Lord for our mother the earth . . .
Praised be my Lord for our sister the death of the
    body. . . .

*From 'The Canticle of the Sun' by St Francis of Assisi, 1181–1226
(Appleton, 1985)*

For I will consider my cat, Jeoffry.
For he is the servant of the Living God, duly and daily
    serving him.
For at the first glance of the glory of God in the East he
    worships in his way. . . .
For God has blessed him in the variety of his movements.
For there is nothing sweeter than his peace when at rest.
For I am possessed of a cat, surpassing in beauty, from
    whom I take
        occasion to bless Almighty God.

*From 'Jubilate Agno' by Christopher Smart, 1722–71, as adapted
by Benjamin Britten*

The house has been far out at sea all night,
The woods crashing through darkness, the booming hills,
Winds stampeding the fields under the window
Floundering black astride and blinding wet

Till day rose; then under an orange sky
The hills had new places, and wind wielded
Blade-light, luminous black and emerald,
Flexing like the lens of a mad eye.

From 'Wind' by Ted Hughes, 1930–98

Remove the green cover from the soil of Central Africa and it becomes a brick-hard, everlasting laterite. Cut down the forests, overgraze the grass, and productive land turns to desert. Overload the waters with sewage or nutrients and algae consumes its oxygen, fish die and produce stinking gas as they decompose.... They teach surely one thing above all – a need for extreme caution, a sense of the appalling vastness and complexity of the forces that can be unleashed and of the egg-shell delicacy of the arrangements that can be upset.

Barbara Ward, 1914–81, and René Dubos, 1901–81

Blessed are you, Lord, God of all creation.
Through your goodness we have this bread to offer,
which earth has given and human hands have made.
It will become for us the bread of life.

Blessed are you, Lord, God of all creation.
Through your goodness we have this wine to offer,
fruit of the vine and work of human hands.
It will become our spiritual drink.

Prayers when the Table is prepared at the Eucharist (Silk, 1986)

Sharing in humanity

God, the king of righteousness,
lead us, we pray, in the ways of justice and peace;
inspire us to break down all tyranny and oppression,
to gain for everyone their due reward,
and from everyone their due service;
that each may live for all, and all may care for each,
in the name of Jesus Christ our Lord.

Archbishop William Temple, 1881–1944 (Baker, 1946)

When you reap your harvest in your field and forget a sheaf in the field, you shall not go back to get it; it shall be left for the alien, the orphan, and the widow, so that the Lord your God may bless you in all your undertakings. . . . Remember that you were a slave in the land of Egypt.

Deuteronomy 24. 19, 22

Because there is one bread, we who are many are one body, for we all partake of the one bread.

1 Corinthians 10. 17

There is no longer Jew or Greek, there is no longer slave or free, there is no longer male and female; for all of you are one in Christ Jesus.

Galatians 3. 28

Ye that do truly and earnestly repent you of your sins, and are in love and charity with your neighbours, and intend to lead a new life. . . . Draw near with faith.

From Holy Communion, BCP and CW

All guests are to be received as Christ himself.

Monastic Rule of St Benedict, c. 480–c. 550 (Bettenson, 1963)

Christmas poor

You are the caller
You are the poor
You are the stranger at my door

You are the wanderer
The unfed
You are the homeless
With no bed

You are the man
Driven insane
You are the child
Crying in pain

You are the other who comes to me
If I open to another you're born in me

David Adam, 1936–

The Church is Catholic, universal, so are all her actions; all that she does belongs to all. When she baptizes a child, that action concerns me; for that child is thereby connected to that Head which is my Head too, and engrafted into that body, whereof I am a member. And when she buries a man, that action concerns me. . . . No man is an island, entire of itself; every man is a piece of the continent . . . any man's death diminishes me, because I am involved in mankind; and therefore never send to know for whom the bell tolls; it tolls for thee.

John Donne, 1573–1631 (Hayward, 1945)

We are everlasting debtors to known and unknown men and women. We do not finish breakfast without being dependent on more than half the world. When we arise in the morning, we go into the bathroom where we reach for a sponge which is provided for us by a Pacific Islander. We reach for soap which is created for us by a Frenchman. The towel is provided by a Turk. Then at the table we drink coffee which is provided for us by a South American, or tea by a Chinese, or cocoa by a West African. Before we leave for our jobs we are beholden to more than half the world.

Martin Luther King, 1929–68

Parliaments, town councils, judges, magistrates, have their place in the Divine order. The Christian man is not released from the obligations of citizenship; to him these obligations are strengthened by new sanctions, and for the manner in which he discharges them he will have to give account at the judgment seat of God. 'Render to Caesar the things that are Caesar's.' The precept was suggested by a question about tribute. In its original reference it enforced the duty of paying taxes ... Paul makes tax-paying a religious duty.

R. W. Dale, 1829–95

What life have you if you have not life together?
There is no life that is not in community,
And no community not lived in praise of God.
Even the anchorite who meditates alone,
For whom the days and nights repeat the praise of God,
Prays for the Church, the Body of Christ incarnate.
And now you live dispersed on ribbon roads,
And no man knows or cares who is his neighbour
Unless his neighbour makes too much disturbance,
But all dash to and fro in motor cars,
Familiar with the roads and settled nowhere.

From Choruses from 'The Rock' by T. S. Eliot, 1888–1965

I need to point out that in the Old Testament God was first experienced by the Israelites in the event of the exodus. They were at the time just a rabble of slaves. They did not encounter God in some religious event such as a sacrifice or at worship; he revealed himself in helping them to escape from bondage, and what could be more political than helping captives to escape? And it is this political event of the exodus which becomes the founding event of the people of God. ... And when God redeemed us in our Lord and Saviour Jesus Christ it was not through a religious event. No, it was through an act of execution used against common criminals.

Archbishop Desmond Tutu, 1931–

Believe me, it was often thus:
In solitary cells, on winter nights
A sudden sense of joy and warmth
And a resounding note of love.
And then, unsleeping, I would know
A-huddle by an icy wall
Someone is thinking of me now,
Petitioning the Lord for me.

From 'Believe me' by Irina Ratushinskaya, 1954–, a prisoner of conscience, written the day after being released from a Soviet prison in 1986.

One of the crowd went up,
And knelt before the Paten and the Cup,
Received the Lord, returned in peace, and prayed
Close to my side. Then in my heart I said:

'O Christ, in this man's life –
This stranger who is Thine – in all his strife,
All his felicity, his good and ill,
In the assaulted stronghold of his will,

'I do confess Thee here,
Alive within this life; I know Thee near
Within this lonely conscience, closed away
Within this brother's solitary day.

'Christ in his unknown heart,
His intellect unknown – this love, this art,
This battle and this peace, this destiny
That I shall never know, look upon me!

'Christ in his numbered breath,
Christ in his beating heart and in his death,
Christ in his mystery! From that secret place
And from that separate dwelling, give me grace!'

Alice Meynell (1847–1922)

Lord, make us instruments of your peace.
Where there is hatred, let us sow love;
where there is injury, pardon;
where there is discord, union;
where there is doubt, faith;
where there is despair, hope;
where there is darkness, light;
where there is sadness, joy.

A Franciscan prayer

Encountering other traditions

Lead me from death to life, from falsehood to truth.
Lead me from despair to hope, from fear to trust.
Lead me from hate to love, from war to peace.
Let peace fill our heart, our world, our universe.

The prayer for peace by Satish Kumar, 1936– (Appleton, 1985)

Long ago God spoke to our ancestors in many and various ways
by the prophets, but in these last days he has spoken to us by a
Son, whom he appointed heir of all things, through whom he also
created the worlds. He is the reflection of God's glory and the
exact imprint of God's very being, and he sustains all things by his
powerful word.

Hebrews 1. 1–3

It was there from the beginning; we have heard it; we have seen it
with our own eyes; we looked upon it, and felt it with our own
hands: our theme is the Word which gives life. This life was made
visible; we have seen it and bear our testimony; we declare to you
the eternal life which was with the Father and was made visible to
us.

1 John 1. 1–2 (REB)

When we approach the man of another faith than our own it will
be in a spirit of expectancy to find how God has been speaking to
him and what new understandings of the grace and love of God
we may ourselves discover in this encounter. Our first task in
approaching another people, another culture, another religion, is
to take off our shoes, for the place we are approaching is holy. Else
we may find ourselves treading on men's dreams. More serious still,
we may forget that God was here before our arrival.

*Max Warren, 1904–77, one-time General Secretary of the Church
Missionary Society (Appleton, 1961)*

The search for peace between the world faiths is one of the most
urgent tasks facing humankind. . . . What then needs to be done?

What can we do? What new relationships should we be seeking? Allow me to answer these questions by way of four attitude-transforming statements: friendship not hostility; understanding not ignorance; reciprocity not exclusivism; cooperation not confrontation. . . . 'Can believers who really believe passionately in their hearts that theirs is a missionary faith which calls people to holiness and truth, really be committed to dialogue?' I answer: 'Yes, we can.' It is possible, as long as we are willing to listen to others, are committed to peace and wish to understand.

Archbishop George Carey, 1935–, speaking at Al-Azhar, the historic Islamic university in Cairo, 1995

It is so easy to speak with people who share your faith, and so hard to communicate with those who don't. But slowly I discovered that talking across the fences that divide us is important. Not only because it helps us understand each other and our differences, but also because it helps us understand ourselves. We find out what we share and also what we uniquely own.

I also made a discovery. With the transition of Britain from a strong common culture to a more fragmented, segmented and pluralised one, we suddenly find that we are *all* members of a minority group, practising Christians no less than practising Jews. This is not a bad thing, because it means that paradoxically as we become more diverse we discover more areas of common experience. The problems of Christians, Jews, Muslims, Sikhs, Hindus and others in trying to preserve their values and hand them on to their children become more not less, alike. . . .

The Jewish sages noted that on only one occasion does the Hebrew Bible command us to love our neighbour, but in thirty-seven places it commands us to love the stranger. Our neighbour is one we love because he is like ourselves. The stranger is one we are taught to love precisely because he is *not* like ourselves.

Jonathan Sacks, Chief Rabbi, 1948–

Pain

Almighty God,
whose most dear Son went not up to joy
   but first he suffered pain,
and entered not into glory before he was crucified:
mercifully grant that we, walking in the way of the cross,
may find it none other than the way of life and peace;
through Jesus Christ your Son our Lord.

Lent 3, CW

My God, my God, why have you forsaken me,
and are so far from my salvation,
   from the words of my distress?

Psalm 22.1

The Lord is my shepherd;
therefore can I lack nothing.
Though I walk through the valley of the shadow of death,
   I will fear no evil;
for you are with me;
   your rod and your staff, they comfort me.

Psalm 23. 1, 4

O God, you are my God; eagerly I seek you;
my soul is athirst for you.
My flesh also faints for you,
as in a dry and thirsty land where there is no water.

Psalm 63. 1

The steadfast love of the Lord never ceases, his mercies never come
to an end; they are new every morning; great is your faithfulness.

Lamentations 3. 22–3

Jesus came and stood among them and said, 'Peace be with you.'
After he said this, he showed them his hands and his side.
John 20. 19–20

Jesus clings to God even when utterly empty and burnt out, even
in the most desperate situation, when all prayer dies out and no
words come to his lips.
Hans Küng, 1928–

> Lead, kindly Light, amid the encircling gloom,
>   Lead thou me on;
> The night is dark, and I am far from home,
>   Lead thou me on.
> Keep thou my feet; I do not ask to see
> The distant scene; one step enough for me.
> *John Henry Newman, 1801–90 (NEH)*

Early that morning (and every morning afterwards) I stood in
front of a piece of wall between two barred and grilled high
windows, which was the nearest thing to a cross that I could find
in the cell. I faced it as I would an altar and said what I could
remember of the Mass. Later when I had my Office Book ... I
could read part of an Epistle or Gospel as well, but from the first
morning I said the Creed, and prayed ... and made a short confession; then I said the *Sanctus* by heart and made a spiritual
communion. ... I have always said to people when they are feeling
'down' about their religion that if they can only go through the
motions and do the things that their rule obliges them to, they
will come out all right. This was my experience at this time – not
because I had any conscious feeling of the Presence of God, but
because, by doing what the rest of the Church was doing, I was
joining in something much bigger than myself. Underlying my
panics and weeping-fits and fear, there was a sense of immense
strength upholding me, and surrounding me like a wall. Later, of
course, I found that Christians all over the world, including many
religious communities, had been praying for me.
Gonville ffrench-Beytagh, 1912–91, imprisoned when Dean of Johannesburg for
opposition to apartheid

I believe in the sun, even if it does not shine.
I believe in love, even if I do not feel it.
I believe in God, even if I do not see him.

Written on a wall of the Warsaw ghetto by a young Jew c. 1942
(Küng, 1978)

People who only see me speaking at meetings may be tempted to think that I am mature and well balanced all the time and have no needs. Nothing could be further from the truth. At times I have an overwhelming sense of failure and am deeply distressed. I can get critical, jealous and resentful. Often I hate or condemn myself. . . . When I was depressed once, someone sent me these words: 'Enjoy who you are, my child – my child who has nothing to prove but the depths of your Father's everlasting and unchanging love.' This helped to bring me relief and healing.

David Watson, evangelist, 1933–84

But so I have seen the sun kiss the frozen earth which was bound up with the images of death, and the colder breath of the north. And then the waters break from their enclosures, and melt with joy, and run in useful channels. And the flies do rise again from their little graves in walls, and dance awhile in the air, to tell that there is joy within, and that the great mother of creatures will open the stock of her new refreshment, become useful to mankind and sing praises to her Redeemer. So is the heart of a sorrowful man under the discourses of a wise comforter. He breaks from the despairs of the grave, and the fetters and chains of sorrow. He blesses God, and he blesses thee, and he feels his life returning. For to be miserable is death, but nothing is life but to be comforted, and God is pleased with no music from below so much as in the thanksgiving songs of relieved widows, of supported orphans, of rejoicing and comforted and thankful persons.

Bishop Jeremy Taylor, 1613–67 (Smith, 1930)

This word 'You will not be overcome' was said very distinctly and firmly. . . . He did not say, 'You will never have a rough passage, you will never be over-strained, you will never feel uncomfortable,' but he *did* say 'You will never be overcome.'

Julian of Norwich, 1342–1416

When the crucified Jesus is called the 'image of the invisible God', the meaning is that *this* is God, and God is like *this*. God is not greater than he is in this humiliation. God is not more glorious than he is in this helplessness. God is not more divine than he is in this humanity.

Jürgen Moltmann, 1926–

God is love: and he enfoldeth
   All the world in one embrace;
With unfailing grasp he holdeth
   Every child of every race.
And when human hearts are breaking
   Under sorrow's iron rod,
Then they find that selfsame aching
   Deep within the heart of God.

From 'God is love' by Timothy Rees CR, 1874–1939 (HAM)

Repentance

Almighty and everlasting God,
you hate nothing that you have made
and forgive the sins of all those who are penitent:
create and make in us new and contrite hearts
that we, worthily lamenting our sins
and acknowledging our wretchedness,
may receive from you, the God of all mercy,
perfect remission and forgiveness;
through Jesus Christ your Son our Lord.

Ash Wednesday, CW

Jesus came to Galilee, proclaiming the good news of God, and saying, 'The time is fulfilled, and the kingdom of God has come near, repent, and believe in the good news.'

Mark 1. 14–15

So he set off and went to his father. But while he was still far off, his father saw him and was filled with compassion; he ran and put his arms around him and kissed him. Then the son said to him, 'Father, I have sinned against heaven and before you; I am no longer worthy to be called your son.' But the father said to his slaves, 'Quickly, bring out a robe – the best one – and put it on him; put a ring on his finger and sandals on his feet. And get the fatted calf and kill it, and let us eat and celebrate; for this son of mine was dead and is alive again; he was lost and is found!'

Luke 15. 20–4

In the evening I went very unwillingly to a society in Aldersgate Street, where one was reading Luther's preface to the Epistle to the Romans. About a quarter before nine, while he was describing the change which God works in the heart through faith in Christ, I felt my heart strangely warmed. I felt I did trust in Christ, Christ alone, for salvation; and an assurance was given me that He had taken away *my* sins, even *mine*, and saved *me* from the law of sin and death.

John Wesley, 1703–91

I see the evil in the blindness and selfishness of all nations . . . I see it in the idolatry of wealth; I see it in the passive acceptance for years of the unemployment of millions, of the ill-housing of millions, of the starvation of millions all over the world; I see it in the bitter nationalism which sets people against people and makes sheer power and domination the be-all and end-all of government.

Bishop George Bell, 1883–1958

A brother who had sinned was turned out of the church by the priest; Father Bessarion got up and went with him saying, 'I too am a sinner.'

Fourth-century Desert Father (Ward, 1975)

About one a.m. on Advent Sunday morning, I had a bad asthmatic attack. In my helplessness, I cried out to God to speak to me. I'm not very good at listening to God, but between one and three a.m. God spoke to me so powerfully and painfully that I have never felt so broken before him (and still do). . . . As the Lord put various names into my mind I began to write letters to about twelve people asking for forgiveness for hurting them, for still being inwardly angry against them – or whatever. It was the most painful pruning and purging I can remember in my entire Christian life.

David Watson, evangelist, 1933–84

I believe that forgiveness is mainly doing something about aggression and retaliation. It's a matter of getting your aggression diverted from someone, or the thought of that person, so that in time your love can flow through and take its place. That piece of work is bound to take time, may even take the rest of one's life, may never be completed in this life. It's a help to realize that forgiveness is a job of that magnitude.

Neville Ward, 1915–92

The ministry of absolution is the ministry by which those who are truly sorry for their sins, and have made free confession of them to God in the presence of the minister, with intention to amend their lives, receive through him the forgiveness of God.

Revised Catechism

I commend to you what is called 'going to confession'. . . . The Church of England offers this way of confession and absolution to those who voluntarily choose it. It is a method thorough, painful, decisive, full of comfort. The priest is no barrier: rather does his ministry enable you to find Christ near in his own vivid forgiveness.

Archbishop Michael Ramsey, 1904–88

Our Lord Jesus Christ, who hath left power to his Church to absolve all sinners who truly repent and believe in him, of his great mercy forgive thee thine offences: And by his authority committed to me, I absolve thee from all thy sins, in the Name of the Father, and of the Son, and of the Holy Ghost. Amen.

The priest's absolution in The Visitation of the Sick, BCP

Dark and cheerless is the morn
   Unaccompanied by thee;
Joyless is the day's return,
   Till thy mercy's beams I see;
Till they inward light impart,
Glad my eyes and warm my heart.

From 'Christ, whose glory fills the skies' by Charles Wesley,
1707–88 (NEH)

Healing

Almighty God, the fountain of all wisdom,
you know our needs before we ask
    and our ignorance in asking;
have compassion on our weakness
    and give us those things
which for our unworthiness we dare not,
and for our blindness we cannot ask,
for the sake of your Son, Jesus Christ our Lord.

CW

Honour physicians for their services, for the Lord created them; for their gift of healing comes from the Most High. . . . The Lord created medicines out of the earth, and the sensible will not despise them.

Ecclesiasticus 38. 1, 2, 4

Are any among you sick? They should call for the elders of the church and have them pray over them, anointing them with oil in the name of the Lord. The prayer of faith will save the sick, and the Lord will raise them up; and anyone who has committed sins will be forgiven. Therefore confess your sins to one another, and pray for one another, so that you may be healed.

James 5. 14–16

The sacramental ministry of healing is the ministry by which God's grace is given for the healing of spirit, mind, and body, in response to faith and prayer, by the laying on of hands, or by anointing with oil.

Revised Catechism

God is never in a hurry. And so we must let go of our neurotic search for quick cures for personality defects and the quest for instant wholeness. God is changing us from glory into glory, it is true. But the change is almost always slow and gradual with the occasional spurt for our encouragement.

Joyce Huggett, 1937–

Listening is an art that must be developed. . . . It needs the full and real presence of people to each other. It is indeed one of the highest forms of hospitality. Why is listening to know through and through such a healing service? Because it makes strangers familiar with the terrain they are travelling through and helps them to discover the way they want to go. . . . Healers are hosts who patiently and carefully listen to the story of the suffering strangers.

Henri Nouwen, 1932–96

Handicapped people remind us that life is not all go-getting and individual achievement. There are more fundamental human values. Handicap demands mutual support, a sense of communal sharing. Handicap fosters compassion and helpfulness, care and concern. It challenges our selfishness and our ambition and sectional loyalties. Society needs handicap.

Frances Young, 1939–, theologian and mother of a severely disabled son

Jesus told us to love our enemies, for by loving them we may turn them into our friends. This applies supremely to the enemy within. For our own worst enemy is always ourselves.

Harry Williams CR, 1919–

Christ leads me through no darker rooms
Than he went through before.

*From 'Lord, it belongs not to my care' by Richard Baxter, 1615–91
(NEH)*

Whoever dwells in the shelter of the Most High
and abides under the shadow of the Almighty,
Shall say to the Lord, 'My refuge and my stronghold,
my God, in whom I put my trust.'

Psalm 91. 1–2

Growing older

O Lord God,
when thou givest to thy servants to endeavour any
    great matter,
grant us also to know that it is not the beginning,
but the continuing of the same unto the end,
until it be thoroughly finished,
which yielded the true glory;
through him who for the finishing of thy work
    laid down his life,
our Redeemer, Jesus Christ.

Based on a prayer of Sir Francis Drake, c. 1545–96
(Milner-White, 1952)

O God, you have taught me since I was young,
and to this day I tell of your wonderful works.
Forsake me not, O God,
    when I am old and grey-headed,
till I make known your deeds to the next generation
    and your power to all that are to come.

Psalm 71. 17–18

There is a happy piquancy in the fact that so often the cheaper
tickets to which we are entitled as OAPs are marked 'Child'. . . .
Indeed, for the retired, it is a ticket to freedom, something of the
long-lost freedom of childhood before too much was expected of
us, when choices were not accompanied by responsibilities. There
is at first, at least, a headiness about being free to do what we
choose rather than what we cannot avoid. . . . [But] there is no use
pretending that, for many of us, retirement has not something of
the sense of bereavement. . . . It can be a time of deep desolation.
Another freedom which comes, as we run the film backward, is the
gradual relinquishment of our accumulated toys. . . . I have to
admit that, for a pilgrim, I had accumulated rather too much
baggage, too many things to watch over. . . . But the OAP ticket
into the freedom of a child is something to savour – time to

dawdle and to stare. Enjoying the *feel* of things and delighting in the smells of spring and the colours of autumn. The excitements of enjoying things for the first time and enjoying them for the last time draw so close together that they become less and less distinguishable.... Perhaps the best bonus of retirement is that it is one stage nearer home.

Bishop Oliver Tomkins, 1908–92

Old age

The seas are quiet when the winds give o'er;
So calm are we when passions are no more ...
The soul's dark cottage, batter'd and decay'd,
Lets in new light through chinks that Time hath made:
Stronger by weakness, wiser men become
As they draw near to their eternal home.
Leaving the old, both worlds at once they view
That stand upon the threshold of the new.

Edmund Waller, 1606–87 (Quiller-Couch, 1939)

Life has its own ways of setting examinations for us, and every ten years or so most of us find ourselves in new situations, which in turn ask new questions of our faith. Around our 'Sixty Plus' we meet a whole group of them – growing older, meeting pain and illness, separation and bereavement, death.... We are here to acknowledge the mysterious wisdom of God who is for ever disturbing, interrupting, breaking the patterns of our human loves so that every handshake, every wave of the hand, every departure, is the reminder that we are strangers and pilgrims and have here no abiding city.

Gordon Rupp, 1910–86

If I cannot work or rise from my chair or my bed, love remains to me; I can pray.

George Congreve SSJE, 1835–1918 (Woodgate, 1956)

Bereavement

O God, who brought us to birth,
and in whose arms we die,
in our grief and shock,
contain and comfort us;
embrace us with your love,
give us hope in our confusion,
and grace to let go into new life,
through Jesus Christ.

Janet Morley, 1951–

Give rest, O Christ, to your servant with the saints:
where sorrow and pain are no more,
neither sighing, but life everlasting.
You are only immortal, the creator and maker of all:
and we are mortal, formed from the dust of the earth,
and unto earth shall we return.
For so you ordained when you created me, saying:
'Dust you are and to dust you shall return.'
All of us go down to the dust,
yet weeping at the grave we make our song:
Alleluia, alleluia, alleluia.
Give rest, O Christ, to your servant with the saints:
where sorrow and pain are no more,
neither sighing, but life everlasting.

The Eastern Orthodox Contakion
from Ministry at the Time of Death, CW

But the souls of the righteous are in the hand of God, and no
torment will ever touch them. In the eyes of the foolish they
seemed to have died, and their departure was thought to be a
disaster, and their going from us to be their destruction; but they
are at peace. . . . Those who trust in him will understand truth, and
the faithful will abide with him in love.

Wisdom 3. 1–3, 9

Do not let your hearts be troubled. Believe in God, believe also in me. In my Father's house there are many dwelling places. If it were not so, would I have told you that I go to prepare a place for you? And if I go and prepare a place for you, I will come again and will take you to myself, so that where I am, there you may be also.

John 14. 1–3

Without any warning, the tears rose up and broke out of her, and Potter sat on his chair, saying nothing, and yet being a comfort to her, taking some of her grief on to himself. She wept as she had never wept before in front of any human being and it was a good thing to do, it was of more value than all the months of solitary mourning. It brought something else to an end.

From In the Springtime of the Year *by Susan Hill, 1942–*

As for my friends, they are not lost:
   The several vessels of thy fleet
Though parted now by tempests tossed,
   Shall safely in the haven meet . . .

Before thy throne we daily meet
   As joint petitioners to thee;
In spirit each the other greet,
   And shall again each other see.

From 'He wants not friends' by Richard Baxter, 1615–91 (NEH)

Preparing for death

Be present, O merciful God,
and protect us through the silent hours of this night,
so that we who are wearied
by the changes and chances of this fleeting world,
may repose upon thy eternal changelessness;
through Jesus Christ our Lord.

From Night Prayer (Compline), CW

Into your hands, O Lord, I commend my spirit.

Save us, O Lord, while waking,
and guard us while sleeping,
that awake we may watch with Christ
and asleep may rest in peace.

From Night Prayer (Compline), CW

Bring us, O Lord God,
at our last awakening into the house and gate of heaven,
to enter into that gate and dwell in that house,
where there shall be no darkness nor dazzling but one
    equal light,
no noise nor silence but one equal music,
no fears nor hopes but one equal possession,
no ends nor beginnings but one equal eternity,
in the habitations of thy majesty and thy glory,
    world without end.

Based on a prayer of John Donne, 1573–1631 (Milner-White, 1952)

We brought nothing into this world, and it is certain we can carry
nothing out.

(1 Timothy 6. 7) Burial Service, BCP

For now we see in a mirror, dimly, but then we will see face to face.
Now I know only in part, but then I will know fully, even as I have
been fully known.

1 Corinthians 13. 12

Then shall the Minister examine whether he repent him truly of his sins, and be in charity with all the world; exhorting him to forgive, from the bottom of his heart, all persons that have offended him; and if he have offended any other, to ask them forgiveness; and where he hath done injury or wrong to any man, that he makes amends to the uttermost of his power. And if he have not before disposed of his goods, let him then be admonished to make his Will. . . . Here shall the sick person be moved to make a special confession of his sins, if he feel his conscience troubled with any weighty matter. After which confession, the Priest shall absolve him (if he humbly and heartily desire it).

Visitation of the Sick, BCP

. . . at that last moment when I feel I am losing hold of myself and am absolutely passive within the hands of the great unknown forces that have formed me; in all those dark moments, O God, grant that I may understand that it is You (provided only my faith is strong enough) who are painfully parting the fibres of my being in order to penetrate to the very marrow of my substance and bear me away within Yourself.

Pierre Teilhard de Chardin SJ, 1881–1955

I said to the man who stood at the Gate of the Year, 'Give me a light that I may tread safely into the unknown.' And he replied, 'Go out into the darkness, and put your hand into the Hand of God. That shall be to you better than light, and safer than a known way.'

Louise Haskins, 1875–1957, quoted by George VI, Christmas 1939
(Wheeler-Bennett, 1958)

Soul of Christ, sanctify me.
Body of Christ, save me.
Blood of Christ, refresh me.
Water from the side of Christ, wash me.
Passion of Christ, strengthen me.
O good Jesus, hear me.
Within your wounds hide me.
Let me never be separated from you.
From the power of darkness defend me.

In the hour of my death, call me
    and bid me come to you,
that with your saints I may praise you
    for ever and ever.

'Anima Christi', thirteenth century

He has set his heart on us, and this is the best hope any of us can
entertain.

Austin Farrer, 1904–68

The day thou gavest, Lord, is ended,
    The darkness falls at thy behest;
To thee our morning hymns ascended,
    Thy praise shall sanctify our rest.

We thank thee that thy Church unsleeping,
    While earth rolls onward into light,
Through all the world her watch is keeping,
    And rests not now by day nor night.

John Ellerton, 1826–93 (NEH)

Go forth upon your journey from this world,
in the name of God the Father almighty who created you;
in the name of Jesus Christ who suffered death for you;
in the name of the Holy Spirit who strengthens you;
in communion with the blessed saints,
and aided by angels and archangels,
and all the armies of the heavenly host.
May your portion this day be in peace,
and your dwelling the heavenly Jerusalem.

From Ministry at the Time of Death, CW

Then I heard in my dream, that all the bells in the City rang again
for joy; and that it was said unto them, 'Enter ye into the joy of
your Lord.' I also heard the men themselves that they sang with a
loud voice saying, 'Blessing, honour, glory, and power be to him
that sitteth upon the throne, and to the Lamb for ever and ever.'
Now just as the Gates were opened to let in the men, I looked in

after them; and behold, the City shone like the sun, the streets also were paved with gold, and in them walked many men with crowns on their heads, palms in their hands, and golden harps to sing praises withal. . . . And after that, they shut up the Gates: which when I had seen, I wished myself among them.

From Pilgrim's Progress *by John Bunyan, 1628–88*

There we shall be still and see; we shall see and we shall love; we shall love and we shall praise. Behold what will be, in the end, without end! For what is our end but to reach that kingdom which has no end?

St Augustine, 354–430

For all that has been – Thanks!
For all that shall be – Yes!
Dag Hammarskjöld, 1905–61

PART FOUR

Sharing in the company

Part Four: Sharing in the company

In Part Four we reflect upon the communal life, teaching and worship of the Church. St Paul described the Church as the Body of Christ and said that through baptism each Christian becomes a limb or organ of it in order to share in a particular way in the ministry of Christ to the world:

> For just as the body is one and has many members, and all the members of the body, though many, are one body, so it is with Christ. For in the one Spirit we were all baptized into one body – Jews or Greeks, slaves or free – and we were all made to drink of one Spirit. . . . Now you are the body of Christ and individually members of it.

1 Corinthians 12. 12–13, 27

> Almighty God,
> you have knit together your elect
> in one communion and fellowship
>   in the mystical body of your Son Christ our Lord:
> grant us grace so to follow your blessed saints
> in all virtuous and godly living
> that we may come to those inexpressible joys
> that you have prepared for those who truly love you;
> through Jesus Christ your Son our Lord.

Collect for All Saints' Day, CW

The word 'company' literally means a group of people who eat bread together. The Acts of the Apostles summarises four features of the life of the early Church: 'They devoted themselves to the apostles' teaching and fellowship, to the breaking of bread and the prayers' (2. 42).

They shared in the **teaching**, in the **communal** life of the Church, in the common meals which included the **Eucharist**, in the regular **prayer** of temple and synagogue. Christians today can follow the same four-fold pattern to nourish their lives in the faith.

Sharing the teaching

Lord of all power and might,
the author and giver of all good things:
graft in our hearts the love of your name,
increase in us true religion,
nourish us with all goodness,
and of your great mercy keep us in the same;
through Jesus Christ your Son our Lord.
Trinity 7, CW

'Believe in God, believe also in me . . . the Advocate, the Holy Spirit, whom the Father will send in my name, will teach you everything, and remind you of all that I have said to you.'
John 14. 1, 26

The bishop makes this statement about the **faith of the Church of England** before ordinations of the clergy and licensing of the clergy, readers and lay workers.

The Church of England is part of the One, Holy, Catholic and Apostolic Church, worshipping the one true God, Father, Son and Holy Spirit. It professes the faith uniquely revealed in the Holy Scriptures and set forth in the catholic creeds, which faith the Church is called upon to proclaim afresh in each generation. Led by the Holy Spirit, it has borne witness to Christian truth in its historic formularies, the Thirty-nine Articles of Religion, *The Book of Common Prayer* and the Ordering of Bishops, Priests and Deacons. In the declaration you are about to make, will you affirm your loyalty to this inheritance of faith as your inspiration and guidance under God in bringing the grace and truth of Christ to this generation and making Him known to those in your care?
The Declaration of Assent and Canon C15 (Preface), CW

The **Bible**, in both the Old and the New Testaments, is the record of God's revelation of himself to mankind through his people

Israel, and above all in his Son, Jesus Christ. The Bible was given to us by the Holy Spirit who first inspired and guided the writers, and then led the Church to accept their writings as Holy Scripture. We should read the Bible with the desire and prayer that through it God will speak to us by his Holy Spirit, and enable us to know him and do his will.

Revised Catechism

Never approach the words or the mysteries that are in the Scriptures without praying and asking for God's help. Say, 'Lord, grant me to feel the power that is in them.' Reckon prayer to be the key that opens the true meaning of the Scriptures.

Isaac of Nineveh, died c. 700 (Clément, 1993)

Blessed Lord,
who caused all holy scriptures
    to be written for our learning:
help us so to hear them,
to read, mark, learn and inwardly digest them
that, through patience, and the comfort of your
    holy word,
we may embrace and for ever hold fast
    the hope of everlasting life,
which you have given us in our Saviour Jesus Christ.

Last after Trinity, CW

The early Church composed two summaries of the Christian faith – the **Nicene** and **Apostles' Creeds**. Already in New Testament times the Church had created short summaries of the faith in the form of hymns. These could also be easily remembered by those being instructed for baptism, for example this, to be found in 1 Timothy 3. 16:

He was revealed in flesh,
    vindicated in spirit,
        seen by angels,
proclaimed among Gentiles,
    believed in throughout the world,
        taken up in glory.

The fuller *Nicene Creed* (so called because much of it was agreed at the Council of Nicaea in AD 325) is recited at the Eucharist. The shorter *Apostles' Creed* (so called because it summarised the apostles' teaching) forms part of Morning and Evening Prayer. It is used also for instruction for baptism and confirmation – it is one of the Key Texts (see p. 6). Bishop David Jenkins has summarised the Christian faith in thirteen carefully chosen words:

God is. He is as he is in Jesus. Therefore there is Hope.

Yet all human words are inadequate to describe the splendour and mystery of God. St Simeon (Philippou, 1964) wrote in the tenth century:

We can know God in the same way a man can see a limitless ocean when he is standing by the shore with a candle, during the night. Do you think he can see very much? Nothing much, scarcely anything. And yet, he can see the water well, he knows that in front of him is the ocean, and that this ocean is enormous and that he cannot contain it all in his gaze. So it is with our knowledge of God.

Archbishop Michael Ramsey reminds us:

Christians do not 'believe in the Creeds', but, with the Creeds to help them, they believe in God.

THE TEN COMMANDMENTS

1 I am the Lord your God: you shall have no other gods but me.
2 You shall not make for yourself any idol.
3 You shall not dishonour the name of the Lord your God.
4 Remember the Sabbath and keep it holy.
5 Honour your father and your mother.
6 You shall not commit murder.
7 You shall not commit adultery.
8 You shall not steal.
9 You shall not bear false witness against your neighbour.
10 You shall not covet anything which belongs to your neighbour.

The *Ten Commandments* arose out of the Jewish experience of God, but Christians have also regarded them as authoritative. Indeed, because they can be applied to all societies, they have a universal significance. When a ruler asked Jesus 'What must I do to inherit eternal life?', Jesus replied by asking him first of all about his observance of the Commandments. Only after that did he challenge him to sell all his goods for the poor (Luke 18. 18–24). Jesus' own 'Summary of the Law' (one of the Key Texts, see p. 4) is composed of two texts from the Old Testament.

Obviously each of the Commandments has to be unpacked and interpreted. For example, Christians do not keep the Jewish Sabbath (the fourth Commandment). Nevertheless this Commandment helps us to reflect about the need to give one day a week a quite different character.

Sharing the fellowship

Almighty and everlasting God,
by whose Spirit the whole body of the Church
   is governed and sanctified:
hear our prayer which we offer for all your faithful people,
that in their vocation and ministry
they may serve you in holiness and truth
to the glory of your name;
through our Lord and Saviour Jesus Christ.

Trinity 5, CW

If then our common life in Christ yields anything to stir the heart, any consolation of love, any participation in the Spirit, any warmth of affection or compassion, fill up my cup of happiness by thinking and feeling alike, with the same love for one another and a common attitude of mind.

Philippians 2. 1–2 (REB)

Jesus said to them again, 'Peace be with you. As the Father has sent me, so I send you.'

John 20. 21

THE CHURCH

The Church is the family of God and the Body of Christ through which he continues his reconciling work among men. Its members on earth enter it by baptism and are one company with those who worship God in heaven. The Church is **One** because, in spite of its divisions, it is one family under one Father whose purpose is to unite all men in Jesus Christ our Lord. The Church is **Holy** because it is set apart by God for himself, through the Holy Spirit. The Church is **Catholic** because it is universal, for all nations and for all time, holding the Christian Faith in its fullness. The Church is **Apostolic** because it is sent to preach the Gospel to the whole world, and receives its divine authority and teaching from Christ through his Apostles. There are these orders of ministers in the Church: **Bishops, Priests, and Deacons**.

Revised Catechism

The **Church of England** is the ancient Church of this land, catholic and reformed. It proclaims and holds fast the doctrine and ministry of the One, Holy, Catholic, and Apostolic Church. The **Anglican Communion** is a family of Churches within the universal Church of Christ, maintaining apostolic doctrine and order and in full communion with one another and with the Sees of Canterbury and York.

Revised Catechism

By a **sacrament** I mean the use of material things as signs and pledges of God's grace, and as a means by which we receive his gifts. The *two parts* of a sacrament are the outward and visible sign, and the inward and spiritual grace. Christ in the Gospel has appointed *two sacraments* for his Church, as needed by all for fullness of life, *Baptism*, and *Holy Communion*. Other *sacramental ministries of grace* are confirmation, ordination, holy matrimony, the ministry of absolution, and the ministry of healing.

Revised Catechism

MISSION

It is always tempting for the Church to retreat into an inward-looking ghetto. . . . So, it is essential that we seize what God-given chances we have to speak up for what we believe in, and to share with others the good news of God's love. . . . And people need to see the gospel and not just hear it.

Archbishop Robert Runcie, 1921–2000

'God so loved the world.' God still loves his world, and as Jesus was sent by the Father so the Church is sent by Jesus, in the name of the Father and in the power of the Holy Spirit (John 20. 21). The mission of the Church is:

1. to proclaim the good news of the kingdom;
2. to teach, baptise and nurture new believers;
3. to respond to human needs by loving service;
4. to seek to transform unjust structures of society.

Lambeth Conference, 1988

And as for you, if you are a Christian, the humility wherewith you put yourself alongside your fellow members in the Church, especially alongside those whom you are inclined to think poorly of, is a part of the humility whereby you may become yourself less a part of the Church's scandal and more a part of the Church's glory.

Archbishop Michael Ramsey, 1904–88

STEWARDSHIP

Yours, Lord, is the greatness, the power,
the glory, the splendour, and the majesty;
for everything in heaven and on earth is yours.
All things come from you,
and of your own do we give you.

At the offerings of the people, Holy Communion, CW

All who believed were together and had all things in common; they would sell their possessions and goods and distribute the proceeds to all, as any had need.

Acts 2. 44–5

Jesus's theme of the Kingdom of God, the calling to the Church to be Catholic, reaching across all human divisions and the doctrine of the Incarnation; they lead me to claim that there is a divine bias to the poor, which should be reflected both in the Church and in the secular world. . . . Does God not have a word for those who have advantages? He does indeed have a word for all men; it is not always the same word. 'Where a man has been given much, much will be expected of him' (Luke 12. 48). Sometimes His word to the advantaged is that they must surrender their advantage for the sake of the poor.

Bishop David Sheppard, 1929–

Sharing the Eucharist

Lord Jesus Christ,
we thank you that in this wonderful sacrament
you have given us the memorial of your passion:
grant us so to reverence the sacred mysteries
    of your body and blood
that we may know within ourselves
and show forth in our lives
the fruit of your redemption,
for you are alive and reign, now and for ever.

Maundy Thursday, CW

For I received from the Lord what I also handed on to you, that the Lord Jesus on the night when he was betrayed took a loaf of bread, and when he had given thanks, he broke it and said, 'This is my body that is for you. Do this in remembrance of me.' In the same way he took the cup also, after supper, saying, 'This cup is the new covenant in my blood. Do this, as often as you drink it, in remembrance of me.' For as often as you eat this bread and drink the cup, you proclaim the Lord's death until he comes.

1 Corinthians 11. 23–6

THE EUCHARIST IN THE EARLY CHURCH

At the Eucharist, offer the eucharistic prayer in this way. Begin with the chalice: 'We give thanks to you, our Father, for the holy Vine of your servant David, which you have made known to us through your servant Jesus.'

Glory be to you, world without end.

Then over the particles of bread: 'We give thanks to you, our Father, for the life and knowledge you have made known to us through your servant Jesus.'

Glory be to you, world without end.

'As this broken bread, once dispersed over the hills, was brought together and became one loaf, so may your Church be brought together from the ends of the earth into your kingdom.'

From The Didache *or* Teaching of the Twelve Apostles, *c. 100 (Staniforth, 1968)*

Holy Communion is the sacrament in which, according to Christ's command, we make continual remembrance of him, his passion, death, and resurrection, until his coming again, and in which we thankfully receive the benefits of his sacrifice. It is, therefore, called the **Eucharist**, the Church's sacrifice of praise and thanksgiving; and also the **Lord's Supper**, the meal of fellowship which unites us to Christ and to the whole Church.

Revised Catechism

The *outward and visible sign* in Holy Communion is bread and wine given and received as the Lord commanded. The *inward and spiritual gift* in Holy Communion is the Body and Blood of Christ, truly and indeed given by him and received by the faithful. Receiving the *Body and Blood* of Christ means receiving the life of Christ himself, who was crucified and rose again, and is now alive for evermore.

Revised Catechism

Was ever another command so obeyed? For century after century, spreading slowly to every continent and country and among every race on earth, this action has been done, in every conceivable human circumstance, for every conceivable human need from infancy and before it to extreme old age and after it, from the pinnacles of earthly greatness to the refuge of fugitives in the caves and dens of the earth. . . . And best of all, week by week and month by month, on a hundred thousand successive Sundays, faithfully, unfailingly, across all the parishes of Christendom, the pastors have done this just to *make* . . . the holy common people of God.

Dom Gregory Dix, 1901–52

BEFORE COMMUNION

Lord, this is thy feast,
 prepared by thy longing,
 spread at thy command,
 attended at thine invitation,
 blessed by thine own Word,
 distributed by thine own hand,
 the undying memorial of thy sacrifice upon
  the Cross,
 the full gift of thine everlasting love,
 and its perpetuation till time shall end . . .
So may we come, O Lord, to thy Table; Lord Jesus,
 come to us.

Eric Milner-White, 1884–1963

AFTER COMMUNION

Bless the Lord, O my soul,
and all that is within me bless his holy name.

Psalm 103. 1

Jesus said 'I am the vine, you are the branches'.
May we so dwell in him as he dwells in us.

John 15. 5

Love bade me welcome; yet my soul drew back,
   Guilty of dust and sin.
But quick-ey'd Love, observing me grow slack
   From my first entrance in,
Drew nearer to me, sweetly questioning
   If I lack'd any thing.

'A guest,' I answer'd, 'worthy to be here':
   Love said, 'You shall be he.'
'I, the unkind, ungrateful? Ah, my dear,
   I cannot look on Thee.'
Love took my hand, and smiling did reply,
   'Who made the eyes but I?'

'Truth, Lord; but I have marr'd them; let my shame
    Go where it doth deserve.'
'And know you not,' says Love, 'Who bore the blame?'
    'My dear, then I will serve.'
'You must sit down,' says Love, 'and taste My meat.'
    So I did sit and eat.

George Herbert (1593–1633)

Glory be to thee, O adorable Jesus, who under the outward and visible part, the Bread and Wine, things obvious and easily prepared . . . dost communicate to our souls the mystery of divine love, the inward and invisible grace, thy own most blessed Body and Blood, which are verily and indeed taken and received by the faithful in thy supper, for which all love and glory be to thee. . . .

Lord, what need I labour in vain to search out the manner of thy mysterious presence in the sacrament, when my Love assures me thou art there? All the faithful who approach thee with prepared hearts, they well know thou art there; they feel the virtue of divine love going out of thee, to heal their infirmities and to enflame their affections, for which all love, all glory be to thee.

Bishop Thomas Ken, 1637–1711 (More and Cross, 1935)

Sharing the prayers

Almighty and everlasting God,
you are always more ready to hear than we to pray
and to give more than either we desire or deserve:
pour down upon us the abundance of your mercy,
forgiving us those things of which our conscience is afraid
and giving us those good things
     which we are not worthy to ask
save through the merits and mediation
of Jesus Christ your Son our Lord.
Trinity 12, CW

My heart tells of your word, 'Seek my face.'
Your face, Lord, will I seek.
Psalm 27. 10

In the morning, while it was still very dark, Jesus got up and went out to a deserted place, and there he prayed.
Mark 1. 35

I can do these things only by the help of God and through his **grace**. By God's grace I mean that God himself acts in Jesus Christ to forgive, inspire, and strengthen me by his Holy Spirit. I receive these gifts of God's grace within the fellowship of the Church, when I worship and pray, when I read the Bible, when I receive the Sacraments, and as I live my daily life to his glory.
Revised Catechism

A relationship between two people develops by many different means – by talking and listening, by being silent together, by sharing tasks, by expressing enthusiasms, hopes and fears, by caring for the needs of other people, through laughter and anger, through conflict and harmony, by saying 'Sorry' and 'Thank you'. It is rather like that with God, for Jesus puts a human face on God and makes him believable. However, no relationship develops if it is left to chance, so we need to make a regular time for prayer each day. Remember the words of Jesus: 'whenever you pray, go into your room and shut the door' (Matthew 6. 6).

For many it is a help to have a visual focus for prayer – a lighted candle, an icon or a crucifix. Some worship God bodily by making the sign of the cross, by raising their arms in praise or by praying with the rhythm of their breathing. Some pray through singing and music. Many go regularly for a day or more to a monastery, convent or other house of prayer. However, whether we pray alone or with others we always pray as part of the believing community. The type of prayer known as **the office** reminds us of this (see p. 11).

Send the Holy Spirit on your people
and gather into one in your kingdom
all who share this one bread and one cup,
so that we, in the company of all the saints,
may praise and glorify you for ever,
through him from whom all good things come,
Jesus Christ our Lord.
Eucharistic Prayer B, CW

Our prayer might follow the pattern of the letters of the word **PACTS**: *P* – Pause; *A* – Adore; *C* – Confess; *T* – Thank; *S* – Supplicate (pray for others).

In **meditation**, with the help of the Spirit, we use our imaginations to ruminate on a passage from the Bible or the liturgy, a hymn or perhaps a recent experience. It is good to prepare for the Sunday Eucharist by meditating on the set readings beforehand. We can *picture* the scene; *ponder* its meaning; *promise* to carry out what we have learned. Remember how 'Mary treasured all these words and pondered them in her heart' (Luke 2. 19).

In recent years some Anglicans and Free Church people have discovered how valuable the **rosary** can be, either in its traditional form or in a modified pattern. Through it we can enter more deeply into fifteen scenes or themes of the New Testament. Explanatory booklets about the rosary are available at church bookshops. *Reconsidering the Rosary* by Anthony Vine (Grove Books, 1991) is particularly helpful.

In the **prayer of silence** we rest in God without words, or perhaps with just a couple of words like 'Our Father' gently repeated as we breathe slowly in and out. Anthony Bloom, the Russian Archbishop, tells how an old lady complained to him that she had no sense of God's presence. When he discovered she had been talking all the time she prayed, he suggested that she should sit in silence in her room for fifteen minutes each day and knit before God. She then discovered a presence at the heart of the silence.

Sometimes we have to **struggle** in prayer – with a problem, with a doubt, with suffering, with God himself. Jacob wrestled all night and was blessed because he struggled (Genesis 32. 24–31). Jeremiah and Mary both expressed their doubts when God called them (Jeremiah 1. 4–9; Luke 1. 26–35). Job argued at length with God about the suffering and injustice of the world. Sometimes God seems to 'stand so far off' (Psalm 10. 1). Perhaps God is asking us to pray not for what we feel we get out of it, but to learn to give time and attention to him for his sake alone. In this way God draws us out of being preoccupied with ourselves and our feelings to become centred upon him and his kingdom.

Merciful God,
you have prepared for those who love you
such good things as pass our understanding:
pour into our hearts such love toward you
that we, loving you in and above all things,
may obtain your promises,
which exceed all that we can desire;
through Jesus Christ your Son our Lord.
Trinity 6, CW

List of sources

David Adam, *The Edge of Glory*, SPCK, 1985.
George Appleton, *On the Eightfold Path* (Preface, M. Warren), SCM, 1961.
George Appleton (ed.), *The Oxford Book of Prayer*, OUP, 1985.
St Augustine, *Confessions*, trans. R. S. Pine-Coffin, Penguin, 1961.
St Augustine, *The City of God*, trans. H. Bettenson, Penguin, 1972.
A. E. Baker (ed.), *William Temple and his Message*, Penguin, 1946.
John Barton, *Love Unknown*, SPCK, 1990.
G. K. A. Bell, *The Church and Humanity*, Longmans, 1946.
Henry Bettenson (ed.), *Documents of the Christian Church*, OUP, 1963.
Anthony Bloom, *Living Prayer*, DLT, 1966.
Lionel Blue, *Bright Blue*, BBC Publications, 1985.
John Bunyan, *Pilgrim's Progress*, Penguin, 1965.
The Canons of the Church of England, Church House Publishing, 5th edn 1993.
Pierre Teilhard de Chardin, *Le Milieu Divin*, Collins, 1960.
Church of England Board for Social Responsibility, The, *Work in Britain Today*, CIO, 1969.
Olivier Clément, *The Roots of Christian Mysticism*, New City, 1993.
Margaret Cropper, *Draw Near*, SPCK, 1935.
R. W. Dale, *The Laws of Christ for Common Life*, Hodder & Stoughton, 1884.
C. Day Lewis, *The Complete Poems*, Sinclair-Stevenson, 1992.
Gregory Dix OSB, *The Shape of the Liturgy*, Dacre Press, 1945.
John Donne, Satire III, in *Poems*, Everyman, J. M. Dent, 1947.
George Eliot, *Adam Bede*, Everyman, J. M. Dent, 1951.
T. S. Eliot, *Collected Poems 1909–1935*, Faber and Faber, 1936.
Austin Farrer, *Said or Sung*, Faith Press, 1960.
Austin Farrer, *The End of Man*, SPCK, 1973.
Gonville ffrench-Beytagh, *Encountering Darkness*, Collins, 1973.
Mark Gibbs and Ralph Morton, *God's Frozen People*, Fontana, 1964.
Michele Guinness (ed.), *Tapestry of Voices*, SPCK, 1993.
Dag Hammarskjöld, *Markings*, Faber and Faber, 1964.
John Hayward (ed.), *John Donne: Complete Poetry and Selected Prose*, Nonesuch Press, 1945.
Christopher Herbert (ed.), *Pocket Prayers*, National Society/Church House Publishing, 1993.
George Herbert, *The Poems*, OUP, 1947.

Susan Hill, *In the Springtime of the Year*, Penguin, 1977.

Joyce Huggett, *Listening to Others*, Hodder & Stoughton, 1988.

Joyce Huggett, 'How I pray', *The Tablet*, 6 March 1993.

Ted Hughes, *Selected Poems*, Faber and Faber, 1982.

Julian of Norwich, *Revelations of Divine Love*, trans. C. Wolters, Penguin, 1973.

Kenneth CGA (ed.), *From the Fathers to the Churches*, Collins, 1983.

Martin Luther King, *Strength to Love*, Fontana, 1969.

Hans Küng, *On Being a Christian*, Fount, 1978.

The Lambeth Conference 1988, *The Truth Shall Make You Free*, Church House Publishing, 1988.

C. S. Lewis, *The Four Loves*, Fontana, 1963.

A. Mackey (ed.), *The Collected Works of G. K. Chesterton*, vol. 10, Ignatius Press, 1994.

G. R. D. McLean, *Praying with Highland Christians*, SPCK, 1988.

Alice Meynell, *The Poems*, OUP, 1946.

Eric Milner-White, *After the Third Collect*, Mowbray, 1952.

Eric Milner-White, *My God, My Glory*, SPCK, 1959.

Eric Milner-White and G. W. Briggs, *Daily Prayer*, Penguin, 1959.

Jürgen Moltmann, *The Crucified God*, SCM, 1974.

P. E. More and F. L. Cross (eds), *Anglicanism*, SPCK, 1935.

Janet Morley, *All Desires Known*, SPCK, 1992.

Edwin Muir, *An Autobiography*, Hogarth Press, 1954.

Ursula Niebuhr (ed.), *Justice and Mercy*, Harper and Row, 1974.

Henri Nouwen, *Reaching Out*, Fount, 1980.

Helen Oppenheimer, *The Character of Christian Morality*, Faith Press, 1965.

J. Pearson, *An Exposition of the Creed*, William Tegg, 1876.

A. J. Philippou (ed.), *The Orthodox Ethos*, Holywell Press, 1964.

A. Quiller-Couch (ed.), *The Oxford Book of English Verse*, OUP, 1939 edn.

Michael Ramsey, *The Gospel and the Catholic Church*, Longmans, 1956 edn.

Michael Ramsey, *Introducing the Christian Faith*, SCM, 1961.

Irina Ratushinskaya, *Pencil Letter*, Bloodaxe Books, 1988.

Matt Redman, *Led to the Lost: The Soul Survivor Song Book*, 1999.

Robert Runcie, *One Light for One World*, SPCK, 1988.

Gordon Rupp, *The Sixty Plus and other Sermons*, Fount, 1978.

Jonathan Sacks, *Faith in the Future*, Darton, Longman & Todd, 1995.

David Sheppard, *Bias to the Poor*, Hodder & Stoughton, 1983.

David Silk (ed.), *Prayers for Use at the Alternative Services*, Mowbray, 1986.

L. P. Smith (ed.), *The Golden Grove, Selected Passages from the Sermons and Writings of Jeremy Taylor*, OUP, 1930.

M. Staniforth (trans.), *Early Christian Writings*, Penguin, 1968.

R. S. Thomas, *Collected Poems 1945–1990*, J. M. Dent, 1993.

Angela Tilby, *Let There Be Light*, Darton, Longman & Todd, 1989.

Oliver Tomkins, 'Living with retirement', *Fairacres Chronicle*, Summer 1992.

Desmond Tutu, *The Rainbow People of God*, Doubleday, 1994.

Terry Waite, *Footfalls in Memory*, Hodder & Stoughton, 1995.

Benedicta Ward SLG (trans.), *The Sayings of the Desert Fathers*, Mowbray, 1975.

Barbara Ward and René Dubos, *Only One Earth*, Penguin, 1972.

Neville Ward, *Five for Sorrow, Ten for Joy*, Epworth, 1971.

Neville Ward, *Enquiring Within*, Epworth, 1988.

Timothy Ware (ed.), *The Art of Prayer, An Orthodox Anthology*, Faber and Faber, 1966.

J. Watson (ed.), *Through the Year with David Watson*, Hodder & Stoughton, 1982.

David Watson, *Fear No Evil*, Hodder & Stoughton, 1984.

John Wesley, *The Journal of John Wesley*, Everyman Edition, n.d., vol. 1.

J. Wheeler-Bennett, *King George VI*, Macmillan, 1958.

Harry Williams CR, *True Resurrection*, Mitchell Beazley, 1972.

Harry Williams CR, *Tensions*, Mitchell Beazley, 1976.

M. V. Woodgate, *Father Congreve of Cowley*, SPCK, 1956.

Frances Young, *Face to Face*, T. & T. Clark, 1990.

List of liturgical sources

An Anglican Prayer Book 1989, Church of the Province of Southern Africa.

The Book of Common Prayer 1662, Cambridge University Press.

Celebrating Common Prayer, A Version of the Daily Office SSF, Mowbray, 1992.

Common Worship: Services and Prayers for the Church of England, CHP, 2000.

The Form of Solemnization of Matrimony, 1966.

Prime and Hours, Mowbray, 1961.

The Revised Catechism, SPCK, 1962.

Acknowledgements

The compilers and publishers gratefully acknowledge permission to reproduce copyright material in this book, as indicated in the list below. Every effort has been made to trace and contact copyright owners. If there are any inadvertent omissions in the acknowledgements we apologise to those concerned.

The text of the Book of Common Prayer is the property of the Crown in perpetuity; material from the Book of Common Prayer (some in adapted form) as reproduced in *Common Worship: Services and Prayers for the Church of England* (Church House Publishing, 2000) is reproduced by permission of the publishers.

English translation of Benedictus, Magnificat, Agnus Dei and Nunc Dimittis, are based on (or adapted from) *Praying Together* © 1988.

The Collects for Lent 5 and Epiphany 2 from *Common Worship: Services and Prayers for the Church of England* (Church House Publishing, 2000) taken from *An Anglican Prayer Book*, 1989 © The Provincial Trustees of the Church of the Province of Southern Africa. Used by permission of the publishers.

Other extracts from *Common Worship: Initiation Services* (Church House Publishing, 1998), *Common Worship: Services and Prayers for the Church of England* (Church House Publishing, 2000) and *Common Worship: Pastoral Services* (Church House Publishing, 2000) are copyright © The Archbishops' Council and are used by permission.

Bloodaxe Books: Irina Ratushinskaya, *Pencil Letter*, 75.

Church of the Province of Southern Africa: *An Anglican Prayer Book 1989*, 69.

English Language Liturgical Commission for the English translation of Benedictus, Magnificat, Agnus Dei and Nunc Dimittis, based on (or adapted from) *Praying Together* © 1988. Reproduced by permission of the publisher.

J. M. Dent: R. S. Thomas, *Collected Poems 1945–1990*, 67.

The Estate of C. Day Lewis: 'Walking away', 64.

Faber and Faber Ltd: T. S. Eliot, *Collected Poems 1909–1962*, 74; Dag Hammarskjöld, *Markings*, 95; Ted Hughes, *The Hawk in the Rain*, 71.

International Committee on English in the Liturgy, Inc: *The Roman Missal* © 1973. All rights reserved, 71.

Matt Redman: 'Now to Live the Life', 29. Copyright © 1997 Kingsway's Thankyou Music, PO Box 75, Eastbourne, East Sussex BN23 6NW, UK. Used by permission.

Satish Kumar: 77.

Mowbray, an imprint of Cassell plc: Timothy Rees, 'God is love', 82; Eric Milner-White, *After the Third Collect*, 88, 92.

Ursula Niebuhr on behalf of Reinhold Niebuhr (1943): 68.

The Right Reverend Peter Nott, Bishop of Norwich: ii.

SPCK: David Adam, *The Edge of Glory*, 67, 73; Margaret Cropper, *Draw Near*, 66; G. R. D. McLean, *Praying with Highland Christians*, 51; Eric Milner-White, *My God, My Glory*, 110; Janet Morley, *All Desires Known*, 63, 90.

Kenneth Stevenson and Colin Bradley: 37.

A. P. Watt Ltd on behalf of the Royal Literary Fund: A. Mackey (ed.) *The Collected Works of G. K. Chesterton*, vol. 10, 68.

Subject index

Author index

Index of first lines and titles of familiar passages

The Christian year

The Seasons of the Christian Year

		Feast of Epiphany	Presentation of Christ			Ash Wednesday	Good Friday
Advent	**Christmas** Christmas Day	**Epiphany**		**Sundays before Lent**		**Lent**	

The Christian year is like a journey – a journey we make as we walk the way of Christ. The *Sundays* of the year are milestones or markers along the way and the *Festivals* stand out as peaks of the hills to which we are heading. The *Seasons* define the sort of terrain which lies ahead. They form two groups. The first leads us through the coming of Christ. During *Advent* we climb towards the *Christmas* celebrations of Christ's presence amongst us, always with an eye searching for the distant horizon of Christ's coming at the end of time. From Christmas we travel through *Epiphany* as we see Christ revealed before us and then find this stage of the journey coming to an end on the *Day of the Presentation* as we discover that the Christ child, the light of the nations, is destined to suffer for all people.

The second group of seasons takes us through the saving events of Jesus' dying, rising, ascending and giving of the Spirit. A bridge between the two is provided by some Sundays which prepare us for the season of *Lent*. From *Ash Wednesday* it is clear that the path is pointing towards the passion of Christ. Towards the end of Lent each step is in the shadow of the cross and on *Good Friday* we stand at its foot.

Easter Sunday				All Saints' Day	
	Ascension Day	Pentecost	Trinity Sunday		Christ the King
Easter			**Sundays after Trinity**	**Sundays before Advent**	

Then comes the joy of *Easter* as the sun breaks through and we walk in the light of God's victory. Still on the mountain top, the cloud of God's presence gathers Jesus from our sight at *Ascension*, but from the same cloud of glory comes the wind and fire of the Spirit refreshing his followers with the power of his presence at *Pentecost*.

The journey over the next few months may not have the dramatic features of the last few weeks but *Trinity Sunday* calls us to keep travelling the road as bearers of the Spirit and as members of Christ for praise of the Father. As the autumn arrives, the journey moves both to its conclusion and to its new beginning. Advent once again beckons but before we arrive to celebrate, on *All Saints' Day*, those who have walked before us on the way of Christ and then we rejoice in *Christ the King* as we glimpse the kingdom for which we are called to work and pray.